DROPSHIPPING

A Step-By-Step Guide to Make Money Online by Starting Your Own E-Commerce Business on Shopify, Amazon, eBay, Etsy, Facebook, Instagram, Pinterest, and Other Social Medias

By Tom Mckell

DROPSHIPPING

© **Copyright 2021 - All rights reserved.**

The content contained within this book may not be reproduced, duplicated or transmitted without direct written permission from the author or the publisher.

Under no circumstances will any blame or legal responsibility be held against the publisher, or author, for any damages, reparation, or monetary loss due to the information contained within this book, either directly or indirectly.

Legal Notice:

This book is copyright protected. It is only for personal use. You cannot amend, distribute, sell, use, quote or paraphrase any part, or the content within this book, without the consent of the author or publisher.

Disclaimer Notice:

Please note the information contained within this document is for educational and entertainment purposes only. All effort has been executed to present accurate, up to date, reliable, complete information. No warranties of any kind are declared or implied. Readers acknowledge that the author is not engaging in the rendering of legal, financial, medical or professional advice. The content within this book has been derived from various sources. Please consult a licensed professional before attempting any techniques outlined in this book.

By reading this document, the reader agrees that under no circumstances is the author responsible for any losses, direct or indirect, that are incurred as a result of the use of

DROPSHIPPING

information contained within this document, including, but not limited to, errors, omissions, or inaccuracies.

DROPSHIPPING

Table of Contents

Introduction vii
   What Is Dropshipping? vii

Chapter 1: The Advantages And Disadvantages Of Dropshipping 1
   Pros Of Dropshipping 1
   Cons Of Dropshipping 4
   How To Deal With These Issues 6

Chapter 2: Finding The Right Product 8
   Find Products That Sell 8
   Find Product Ideas In Everyday Things 10

Chapter 3: Find Your Unique Supplier 17
   Finding The Best Dropshipping Suppliers 18

Chapter 4: Choosing The Right Platform 24
   Types Of Dropshipping Platforms 25
   Setting Up Your Own Dropshipping Portal 26
   Using A Hosted Platform With Integrated Cms 28
   Factors To Consider When Choosing A Dropshipping Cms .. 29
   Factors To Consider When Choosing A Dropshipping Platform 32

Chapter 5: Marketing Your Product 35
   Know Your Marketing Channels 35
   Facebook Marketing 36
   Facebook Advertising In Your Dropshipping Business 37
   Facebook Ad Structure At A Glance 38

DROPSHIPPING

Facebook Ads Placement For Dropshipping 44
Key Points To Include In A Facebook Ad 44
Summarizing The Steps To Set Up Facebook Ads To Improve Dropshipping Sales 45
Etsy Marketing 47
The Main Techniques Of Etsy Dropshipping 48
The Pros & Cons Of Etsy Dropshipping 49
The Cons 52
How To Dropship Products From Etsy 55
Etsy Faqs For Dropshipping 57
Amazon Marketing 59
Amazon Dropshipping Benefits 60
How To Sell On Amazon 61
Strategies For A Successful Amazon Dropshipping Store 65
Amazon Dropshipping Tools 68
Dropshipping From Amazon To Ebay 70
Pinterest Marketing 70
Why Is Pinterest Marketing Profitable For Dropshipping Business? 71
How To Use Pinterest For Dropshipping Business 74
Instagram Marketing 81
Why Use Instagram Marketing For Dropshipping? 82
How To Create A Dropshipping Business Account On Instagram 84
Why Is Your Instagram Strategy Not Very Effective? ... 85
Tips To Optimize An Instagram Dropshipping Account ... 88
Additional Ways To Market Your Dropshipping Business 91

DROPSHIPPING

Chapter 6: Scaling Your Business 98
    How Is Scaling Different From Growth? 99
    Steps For Scaling Your Dropshipping Business 100
    Actionable Tips To Have A Positive Scaling Process 104
    Challenges That You Might Face While Scaling Your Dropshipping Business 114

Chapter 7: How To Earn More Sources Of Income 122
    Affiliate Marketing 122
    Critical Parameters To Succeed In Affiliate Marketing 125
    Drop Servicing 127
    What Is The Actual Concept Behind Drop Servicing? 128
    How Drop Servicing Works 129
    How To Get Started With Drop Servicing 130
    Blogging 132
    What Is Blog Marketing? 133
    Why Business Owners Prefer Blog Marketing? 134
    How To Achieve Your Goals In Blog Marketing 135
    Optimize Your Plan To Scale The Right Way 137
    Know The Dropshipping Loopholes 138
    Dropshipping Mistakes You Should Avoid 138

Conclusion 143

DROPSHIPPING

INTRODUCTION

Dropshipping, based on a contemporary business prototype that needs little to no investment. Over the last decade, dropshipping has changed the model of online businesses.

Why is that you ask?

Because it is more approachable now, a phenomenon like Dropshipping bolsters online retail sectors, making it more opportunistic for small-sector entrepreneurs. It's a business model that lowers financial risks while increasing profits.

Now, let's define Dropshipping.

What is Dropshipping?

Dropshipping is a process of assembling and shipping customer orders without the need for a seller to stock the products in his/her warehouse. Instead, the products are shipped directly to the customer through a third-party vendor with the required products. To accomplish this retail fulfillment, the seller purchases the product from the third-party supplier and instructs him to ship the product directly to the customer.

This process negates the direct involvement of the seller in handling the product. You might not know this process, but over one-third of online businesses use this model to fulfill customer requirements. Once the third-party vendor gets the payment for the required product from the seller, the former takes care of the shipping on his own.

In this eBook, we will teach you why this model is so successful for budding entrepreneurs. We will also explain how it works in relation to various social media platforms and which platform would suit your requirements the most.

We will also dig deep to explain the type of product that is the most lucrative for Dropshipping. Later in this eBook, we will give you a detailed tutorial on how you can scale a successful business out of this business model.

So, let's go deeper into this concept and give your entrepreneurial dream a reality.

CHAPTER 1

THE ADVANTAGES AND DISADVANTAGES OF DROPSHIPPING

After hearing the definition of this phenomenal business model, you must be thinking how awesome this is. For entrepreneurs, it's much less demanding compared to conventional retail fulfillment models.

Let's take a look at a few of its main advantages.

Pros of Dropshipping

As a budding entrepreneur, you will find dropshipping a worthy resource that will not demand that much from you. You do not need to invest in a physical store, bear overhead costs, or stock products. Instead, you have an online marketplace where you buy products from third-party suppliers to sell to your customers.

Your role as a merchant is composed of gaining buyers and processing orders. In other words – you are a middleman or a mediator. Nevertheless, you can make tons of money if your

DROPSHIPPING

approach is in the right direction to sell customer-centric products.

Dropshipping does not involve complicated planning. Here are some pros that can help motivate you to try this business model.

Low Order Fulfilment Expenses

In a conventional retail fulfillment scenario, you will need to have a potential customer's product available in your warehouse. Furthermore, the work will involve organizing, tracking, labeling, packing, and shipping the product to the customer. All of these can incur extra costs that you would have to pay.

Fortunately, you do not have to deal with all such operations in Dropshipping. Instead of you, a third-party seller will take care of all this for you. Your only requirement is to track that your customer receives the order.

As a result, you save loads of money, giving you a commission in the shipment transaction that acts without your direct involvement.

Instant Sales

Conventionally, a merchant first needs to have all the products stocked in his/her warehouse to have them shipped to potential customers. After that, he uses a website for marketing the products. With dropshipping, this is all done for you, so there is no need to worry about storage and shipping.

DROPSHIPPING

With dropshipping, you negate this disadvantage by marketing a specific product instantly because you target products that are already available through another seller. That seller is the one who is managing all the products at his/her warehouse.

Low Inventory Costs

You barely require any storage for products, as you are selling products owned by someone else. That limits your expenses, allowing you to create a low-risk business.

Inventory costs are one of the highest expenses for retailers, as you need to spend money for a warehouse and on the products. When you stock products, you often have to deal with an obsolete inventory, which forces you to reduce the stock. Otherwise, you might have to deal with limited inventory – causing a loss of revenue or stock that runs out.

With dropshipping, you avoid all such hassles – focusing only on increasing your clientele and improving your brand reputation.

More Diversification of Products

With dropshipping, you do not have to worry about marketing one or two products because you do not own any of them. You are offering products from various third-party vendors. This way, you have the benefit of offering a broad range of products to your customers.

More options for customers, higher opportunities to make more money!

DROPSHIPPING

And the best part is that you do not have to arrange any of these goods per se. Dropshipping lets you have the fruit grown on someone else's trees.

Risk-Free Testing

When you add new products to your inventory, you should note that there is always a risk of a product failing to meet your target customers' standards. It often gets tricky to understand what customers expect. This can be a risky business if you are trying to market and sell products to buyers through a traditional eCommerce model.

In dropshipping, you do not need to own anything or make heavy investments in products. This gives you the opportunity to test various products to see which one's click with your customers. Once you find that sweet spot, you are good to invest in that particular product that your buyers like.

So, you save a lot without risking your valuable money.

<u>Cons of Dropshipping</u>

Of course, you will find drawbacks to this business model as well. Let's look at how dropshipping can be a disadvantage in the business world.

Complicated When Working with Multiple Sellers

Things are somewhat easier as long as you deal with a single seller who provide your customers with all their needed products, but when you work with multiple third-party suppliers, things get complicated.

DROPSHIPPING

With multiple sellers, you will need to keep track of every order, and each of these sellers may also have their own ways of processing, billing, and shipping orders. This can also lead to more time to ship products to your customers because you have to wait for the seller to ship the order to your customer. Uniformity helps your business.

Things can get even more complicated when the seller deals with multiple mediators like you, fulfilling orders for them simultaneously.

Limited Control Over Order Fulfilment

As sellers are the ones handling all the shipping, and you barely have any involvement in the handling and shipping of the product to your customers. This often leads to delays in deliveries, mismatched orders, or low-quality products.

This can lead to a dissatisfied customer who may not be willing to buy from you in the future, as he deals with you directly rather than the seller. So, you have to bear the profit or loss of the final settlement.

So, one of the key areas to focus on when starting this business is to make sure you do business with the best suppliers in the market.

Less Profit

Dropshipping requires you to sell more if you want to earn more profit. Naturally, you are adding a commission over the product price to sell it to a customer. The buyer could have got the same product from the same seller at a lower price if

DROPSHIPPING

he/she omits your involvement from the deal. But this disadvantage can be reduced if you can sell items in bulk to your customers.

Poor Customer Service

You do not have to deal with the products directly, so you have no idea of what the product might be like in reality. If there is a limited product description about the item, you will find it hard to answer customer queries.

Your only option in such a scenario is to forward questions to the seller, which can take additional time – leading to a frustrated customer. So, there is no real product experience. And the lack of information from you or on your website can harm your brand reputation.

Another common scenario is where you find out that the product you purchased for a customer is out of stock, even though it is shown as being "available." This frequently happens on platforms like eBay, where sellers forget to give you an update that the product is already sold out. As a result, your customer leaves empty-handed with dissatisfaction and skepticism.

How to Deal With These Issues

Looking at the cons may make you feel skeptical about this model but think of it in this way – If various large-scale companies use this model to process orders for their customers, it has to be a profitable model.

DROPSHIPPING

Dropshipping is more about making the right calls, choosing the right products and sellers, so your customer leaves and returns to get more goods from you with a smile. No doubt, you have to work less with the handling, processing, and shipping operations – but you cannot ignore the monitoring duties involved in this business model.

With the right approach, which you will find in the later chapters, you will have a better sense of judgment, improved business skills, and an idea of the platforms best suited for order fulfillment.

CHAPTER 2

FINDING THE RIGHT PRODUCT

Dropshipping gives you a lot of freedom to decide which product to market and sell to your customers. But it's not as easy as it seems. You do need to invest your time and money in a product that customers can find worth buying.

To top it off, that product also needs to be high quality. That involves you looking for top-grade suppliers who can provide you with the product at a favorable price. You have to consider several factors to make sure that your selected item is perfect to sell to your customers.

Once you have a clear idea of which products will be perfect for your dropshipping store, you'll start earning decent profits.

Let's dig deep into what to sell online.

Find Products That Sell

If you can find products that the customers will like, you can make a ton of money, but that process involves planning. Here are some points to keep in mind to find the right products that sell.

DROPSHIPPING

Choose What You Enjoy

To get product ideas, the first thing that may come to your mind is to choose items that you like. You might want to choose products that are related to your hobbies, passions, or interests.

That's one of the easiest choices since you have an idea of what products you are searching for. You don't have to dig deep to understand what products are needed because you are already familiar with them. So, you can do a couple of brainstorming sessions to find such products to sell to your customers.

Use Online Tools

Furthermore, you can use tools like Google Trends to search for the demand for such products in the market. Even if the product is not high in demand on the market, consider it as a possible candidate because you will have less competition in marketing such a product.

Another way you can find products of interest to sell online is by browsing other online stores. It's a common strategy that many businesses apply to keep track of what their competitors are excelling at selling.

Using Social Media Shopping Platforms

You can find plenty of online stores on social media sites too. Just search for a potential product on Pinterest, Instagram, Facebook, etc., and you will have thousands of results lined up to give you various options.

DROPSHIPPING

Many merchants ignore these platforms because they don't know these sites' potential to showcase the trending products worth selling. Why not use all these sources of inspiration to figure out the products that your customers would love?

Satisfying their demand for the perfect product will help you generate more profit with your dropshipping business.

Look for Friend Suggestions

Social media websites are not the only places to brainstorm for finding the perfect products. You can also ask your friends the next time you go out to a social gathering. Ask about potential products that you have researched beforehand on Google Trends or another platform and learn how they feel about them.

You can diversify your search even further by targeting individuals of all ages and groups. A broader range will give you a better scope of earning more.

As a result, you will have more ideas for your dropshipping business that you had not even thought of before.

<u>**Find Product Ideas in Everyday Things**</u>

There are so many products all around you that you need to take note of what people buy. Have a look around you and see all the amenities available to you. Think of which of the products present in shops near you could be a good fit for a dropshipping business.

DROPSHIPPING

You can choose products that people cannot live without. Or you can choose a product that helps simplify things. You can also choose a product that is not easily available to people nearby.

You have plenty of choices, and all you need to do is think clearly about the type of product you want to provide to your customers.

Travel to Help Brainstorm

People often find the best ideas when on the move. Maybe that could work for you too. Travel around and visit various places, and your mind will undeniably come up with loads of product ideas that you can sell to customers.

Make sure you are alert and thinking of opportunities that might knock on your mind's door at any time. Upon adopting such a mindset, you will have no trouble locating products that are a great fit to sell to earn a potential profit every day.

Making Decisions on Top-Selling Products

Once you have an idea of the type of products you can choose for your dropshipping business, you can start narrowing down the list. To do that, you will need to filter them based on the following factors. This lets you form a list of the best products to sell.

Keep in mind that your list is not limited to a shortlist of products. You can always add more to your list and see what is trending among customers, which may be profitable for you, eventually.

DROPSHIPPING

Importing products is fairly easy. The hard part is to know the items that will fill the buyers' needs and sell like hotcakes. The chosen products need to draw the attention of traffic to your online store. Once you find such products, you can market them and sell with additional deals like upselling, cross-selling, etc.

Let's take a look at these factors.

Choose a Niche-Specific Product

The Dropshipping model has added more to the existing eCommerce platforms globally. The trend of niche stores has become popular – prompting several entrepreneurs and organizations to use this successful strategy without competing with large-scale companies.

It does make sense – after all, you avoid fighting large online stores to grab the attention of potential buyers. When you target a specific niche, you omit product categories that are too general or broad. People are already exposed to tons of daily offers in general categories, which may obscure your marketplace from them.

Instead, find niche items that big players skip or do not sell that much.

For example, you might find it hard to sell a normal cap to a customer, but you have more potential at earning profits when selling biking gear to a cyclist.

DROPSHIPPING

Focus on finding a niche that you would love to market. You will have a smaller audience, but every one of them has a higher potential to become a customer.

Narrow Down the Niche Products

Selling niche products is not a new concept in the eCommerce world. Many niche-specific categories already have a clientele that will not move to a new online store that easily.

So, you will need to penetrate even further to filter the niche products if you want to succeed in this business. When you narrow down your product list, excluding items that already have potential customers elsewhere, you increase your chances of targeting the right people.

A good way to filter niche products is by choosing products that are somewhat new. You will need to search among the various categories you are interested in and look for new inventions that emerged on the market but lack a potential audience. Marketing such items can create an authoritative platform for you to sell the items at a decent profit.

You can even target customized products in various niche categories, which are not easily available to the masses. The key is to minimize the product list as much as possible to have the highest chance of selling.

Look for Products That Customers Buy Repeatedly

As we mentioned above, dropshipping has a low-profit margin unless you are selling products in bulk. Even with a low customer base, you can still earn good profits in the long run.

DROPSHIPPING

The key is to choose products that customers buy repeatedly. This is a good strategy to sustain long-term profits.

Choose products that individuals will keep buying over time and strengthen your brand's trustworthiness with them. Products like party supplies, clothing, and cosmetics are good examples of such products that people will need every once in a while.

You can target such goods to them with attractive marketing campaigns, triggering them to buy again. Use personalized emails and newsletters to let customers know that you have the products available and offer them a better deal, if possible. That way, you can create a long-lasting relationship with your buyers.

When a customer lasts with you for a lifetime, you barely need to sell in bulk because you have repeat profit coming your way every time you come up with something new.

Choose a Reasonable Price Range

The Online shopping world is like an ocean where you will find similar products listed by various sellers, and these products will have various prices set for them. You will need to choose products that have an attractive price to lure customers to your online shopping portal.

Here, you can keep in mind a few fundamental rules:

Low price, high conversion rate.

High price, more effort to find a potential buyer.

DROPSHIPPING

You will need to choose a product that has a decent price range. The price should not be too high as it will not encourage buyers. Plus, such a product will barely give you any returns if you do manage to sell it.

Additionally, the price should not be so low that it feels like a cheap product or a rip-off. Customers are intelligent enough to tell what products may be of good quality based on the price.

The chosen price range differs demographically as well. Maybe a particular customer in Europe finds a $20 product expensive compared to a customer living in North America. Do your homework while deciding the products specific to a targeted audience.

Choose Products That Deliver Faster

Customers often rely on services that can offer fast shipment of products. That's one factor that can help you decide the type of product you want to sell. Usually, smaller products can be picked, packed, and shipped faster than bigger ones.

Find niche products that your seller can quickly ship to your customers.

Choose Durable Products

While dropshipping, you will barely have to deal with the products physically. Everything, from choosing, packing, and shipping are taken care of by the seller. You will want the product to reach your customer safely.

DROPSHIPPING

That's why you should choose products that are not fragile because you have little idea of how the product reaches the buyer. Sell products that can withstand heavy blows, the pressure of other goods, etc., while they are being shipped.

When you choose a fragile product, like ornaments, you have no control over the order fulfillment cycle. You do not want to live the memory of an unhappy customer frustrated over a broken product he received from your seller. Such a situation can lose you a potential customer forever.

Find something that is sturdy and durable for long transit journeys.

CHAPTER 3

FIND YOUR UNIQUE SUPPLIER

Besides finding the right product to sell, you need to choose a good supplier too. Without a good third-party seller, you cannot sell effectively even the best product that you can find on the market for your customers.

A major part of your store's credibility will rely on the seller's operations, but finding a capable dropshipper is a daunting task. Often you will find it impossible to find one.

In this chapter, we will help you sort this issue out to find your unique supplier.

The first thing you should know is when to look for suppliers.

Your search should be based on two possible scenarios:

You want both a supplier and a product.

You already have a product in mind, and you just want a supplier now.

Based on these situations, we will discuss the best way to find dropshipping suppliers.

DROPSHIPPING

Finding the Best Dropshipping Suppliers

Remember that a dropshipping seller will need to focus on the order fulfillment on your behalf. It is important that you keep in mind the following points when choosing a potential seller for your business.

Research as Much as Possible

To find the best suppliers, you will need to do lots of research. If you have decided which products you want to sell to your potential clients, you should know which type of sellers to research online. Choose overseas or domestic suppliers based on the product niche you are targeting.

Once you make a list of the potential suppliers, look deeper into their service insights such as delivery cycle, shipping charges, product charges, and customer service.

Talk to Them

You shouldn't just rely on research to know their fundamentals. You also have to speak to them to try to get to know their business acumen. Do they possess the integrity that you are looking for? Will they fulfill the orders for your customers with responsibility and commitment? You can often get an answer to such queries through a simple conversation with such suppliers.

Talking will also build a stronger relationship when you get to know each other. It is a way to build trust so that you and your supplying partner see things in the same way.

DROPSHIPPING

Look for Sellers Who Can Send You Samples

Several suppliers do not mind sending samples to customers. You can use this facility to your advantage. If you have three or four potential suppliers in mind, you can ask for samples from each of them. Test the quality of the sample products, note the delivery time it took for you to receive the items, and other questions that you have in mind.

All the data will help you understand which supplier to choose for a healthy and long-term dropshipping business relationship. If you learn that the potential supplier is also supplying products to a competitor, get a sample from the competitor too.

Test both samples (one from the supplier and one from the competitor) to see if the quality is the same. You can also figure out if the competitor uses the same packaging that you will be using for your customers or some other custom labeling that makes their products and reputation stand out among their rivals.

Target Offline Suppliers

Most sellers who are present online may already be selling products to customers. That's why you should first try searching for potential suppliers offline. Maybe you have local stores that have little idea of how to market their products to customers online.

You can help such suppliers by partnering with them in your business. This gives you another major advantage: the seller

DROPSHIPPING

will be near you, which will let you stay in contact with him/her more effectively.

Look for sellers who deal in niche products of interest to you and your business. You might have to provide them with a good presentation of your idea, so they will understand how they will profit from your business. Otherwise, they would have created an online portal of their own in the first place.

Pitch to Existing Online Suppliers

There are enough fish in the sea for everyone. Suppliers who are already dropshipping for customers can still collaborate with you if you are the right fit for each other. Choosing such a seller is beneficial because you do not have to teach such a person about the business. That saves you a lot of time – letting you move straight to the business if you strike a deal.

Online sellers who lack the skills and experience to manage a dropshipping business could be a good fit for your business. After all, you will become a potential resource to increase their business among your potential audience.

Find Manufacturers That Make Your Niche Products

Instead of targeting sellers, who might be buying products from other sellers, why not target the manufacturers? Companies that manufacture products you want to sell can give you the most profit because you can remove all middlemen from the deal.

But such manufacturers need to have an effective order fulfillment operation, as you will just be placing the order on

DROPSHIPPING

behalf of your customer. The rest of the process involving shipping should be available to the seller.

If you manage to find such a vendor-cum-manufacturer, you can get higher commissions on the products you sell for them.

Choose a Supplier with Professionalism

Professionalism is important in any type of business. If you want to have a professional relationship with your vendor, you should both agree to terms and respect them throughout the cycle. Finding such a seller ensures that your dropshipping business is in credible hands.

A good way to judge a seller for credibility is by working with a seller who does not make you the first offer. You cannot entrust your new business into the hands of such a supplier who has to persuade you to be a part of the business and not the other way around.

Select a Punctual Supplier

Find a supplier that is punctual at processing your orders and shipping them to your customers without delays. Remember, it is not just the orders. Such a seller should also be readily available to answer any queries coming their way. Such vendors should stick to the scheduled shipment cycles to strengthen the relationship further.

Choose a Seller Who Is Nearby

This is not a necessity, but as mentioned earlier, it can be very effective. When you know that the seller is available nearby, you can always monitor their operations and make sure that they fulfill your customer's orders with dedication and punctuality. Knowing your seller is a plus point that enables you to predict future relationships.

But that does not mean a seller located far away cannot give you a good service. It's a matter of how dedicated, honest, and trustworthy they are toward maintaining a good business relationship.

Avoid Choosing a Common Supplier

If the supplier you choose is also supplying to 10 other eCommerce businesses in your area, it can be hard to emerge as a unique dropshipping business. Try choosing a unique supplier who can ensure that you get a one-on-one order fulfillment deal so you can maintain your brand's reputation among end customers.

Find a Seller Who Sticks to a Contract

If a potential supplier asks to maintain a contract or an agreement to fulfill the orders, choose him/her. Such a seller will be beneficial for your business as he/she understands the importance of commitment. That means such a supplier will do his/her best to provide good-quality products for your customers – helping your credibility stay intact.

Choose Wisely

A potential supplier can help make or break your business. You have to make sure that such a seller either knows the

DROPSHIPPING

business properly or is willing to cooperate to learn and grow his/her business with you.

A major part of the order fulfillment process is under the supplier's control. Finding the right one is important to make sure your business and reputation improve in the long run. Finding suppliers who are experienced in this field can be a great addition to your business model. Focus on searching for such sellers first.

If you cannot find them easily, look for the ones who have a sense of professionalism. That way, you know they are willing to learn and dedicate their products and services to your customers without any trouble.

CHAPTER 4

CHOOSING THE RIGHT PLATFORM

Once you have decided on the products to sell and the sellers to work with, you need to look for a reliable dropshipping platform. A dropshipping platform is a place where you sell services and products online through its sales portal.

Finding the right platform for your dropshipping business is significant for a successful business. To do this, you can choose two methods:

1. *Build a website and self-host a dropshipping store.*

2. *Set up a sub-store on a renowned dropshipping marketplace or platform.*

In this chapter, you will learn how to choose the right dropshipping platform, but before that, we will look into the different platforms you can use for dropshipping. We will also look at the factors you can evaluate when picking an ideal marketplace for your business.

DROPSHIPPING

Types of Dropshipping Platforms

Use Pre-Existing Marketplaces for Selling

Dropshippers often select such online platforms because they are resourceful. You do not have to make extra effort to run your business on such portals. All you need to do is set up your business account, upload your products, and start selling. Another plus point here is that you already have an audience visiting the platform to buy items – helping you market and sell your products effectively.

This method is quite easy, but you will still have challenges. For instance, such platforms provide limited customizations for your store. You will have to adjust to the features provided on the platform. You might be looking for features like site integration, fulfillment monitoring, or shipment tracking, but they may all be missing on such a platform. Some platforms have a limit on the number of products you can list on their portal. That, too, can frustrate you.

A restriction in personalization could be a significant downgrade to your branding. Moreover, working through a reputed platform hides your reputation to an extent. For instance, if you use Amazon to sell your products, your customers might tell other potential buyers that they bought the product from Amazon, as they will see Amazon's storefront instead of yours.

When you choose a pre-existing platform, you will also have to compete with other sellers on the same platform. Your pricing strategy will have to be top-notch, so you can attract customers to your storefront. Another downside is that you will have to pay a service fee to the chosen marketplace, which could be 10-15% of the order's price.

Setting Up Your Own Dropshipping Portal

If you open your own online store, you are responsible for everything, which includes complete control over your personal branding. Unlike pre-existing marketplaces, a customer who buys from your website store will mention your website and the store name to other buyers. You don't need to set up your own website from scratch, but you might find building your own store exciting.

On top of that, you can use various plugins and tools of your choice to make your website's user interface interactive and appealing. There will be no limit to what you can add to such a portal which may have been limited to renowned portals. And the best part – you get to keep all the commission *yourself*.

Having your own marketplace with a personal website makes it easier to control the competition. Since your platform for dropshipping will be separate from other dropshippers, you can ask for better prices for your products.

The downside in using this platform is the time, money, and effort you will need to invest in building your website from scratch and coming up with a solid marketing campaign to build your traffic. You will have to work on SEO and other marketing tactics to get a decent rank for your website on the search engine results.

DROPSHIPPING

Using a Self-Hosted Platform

If you are passionate about setting up a marketplace with complete personalization, have a decent amount of money to invest in your business, and have good technical skills, then a self-hosted platform could be a good option for you. This option is suitable for entrepreneurs who want to indulge in a serious money-making business for the long term. For such individuals, such a business is a full-time operation.

If you want to do dropshipping full time and not just set it up as a side income, you too can get a domain name and hosting service for your business. With money to spare, you can hire web designers, content creators, and developers to help you to speed up the project. In no time – you will have your own marketplace ready at your disposal to sell niche products.

Self-hosting platforms will require you to host your website on a server that you own. Even though you have to spend a lot of money on building the site, your profits will give you ample returns to overcome the expenses.

As you gradually get to know the ins and outs of your business, you will upgrade it further with tools, plugins, and upgrades that will give you and your customers a better user experience. As a result, you can have a brand reputation that echoes your name in public without crediting other parties.

Even if you end up with issues, you can look for technical support at various online forums where other dropshippers like you meet and share their queries.

DROPSHIPPING

The Benefit: You will be the boss of your own business without any involvement from big eCommerce platforms. Your profits will be higher without a need to pay a share of your income to large conglomerates.

Using a Hosted Platform with Integrated CMS

If you do not want to involve website designers/developers or do not have the required technical expertise to set up a website for your business, choose a hosted platform with a content management system. Several sites offer plans where you can buy a domain and install eCommerce templates. You just have to fill in your personalized content, products, and descriptions to make your dropshipping business live for your audience.

This method lets you have the raw materials needed to build the site without using too much of your time. The service providers you choose for hosting will give you various pricing plans. You can select one of them to suit your budget. You can start with a basic plan initially if you want to save a little. Once your business shows lucrative results, shift to an advanced plan that can handle your traffic without ruining your site's efficiency.

Talking about customization, most of the time, you will find what you want to add to your dropshipping website. A perk you get with this option is customer support from the service provider to help you whenever you are stuck with a technical issue on the site. This way, you don't have to rely on third-party forums online.

DROPSHIPPING

Furthermore, a content management system lets you add the content in readymade sections on the webpage featuring various dummy products. Just swap existing images and text with a description related to your products.

The only disadvantage we can think of here is that personalization is limited. But you own the website in your brand name with a pre-existing template.

Factors to Consider When Choosing a Dropshipping CMS

Choosing an effective CMS can help your dropshipping business model work wonders. After all, the content management system acts as the backbone for your website to run it with all the features you want.

Do pay heed to the following factors when choosing an effective dropshipping CMS:

- **Provides Desk Performance** – To know if your chosen CMS is a good fit for desk performance, check its reviews. You can also look for forum discussions regarding its efficiency. Also, you can talk to the CMS specialists as a potential buyer to learn about the tool. An ideal CMS comes with a detailed guide that lets you learn about the system in depth. This information can include tutorials, blogs, tips, etc.

- **Features a Simple UI** – A good CMS platform should not be complicated to use. It has to be user-friendly with a simple interface. You can go through the plugins and templates offered by a potential CMS

DROPSHIPPING

platform for your dropshipping store. Browse and test through these resources as a user to understand if the CMS will be worth buying or not.

- **Offers Multi-Channel Support** – You need a CMS that can support inventory data from multiple suppliers simultaneously. Your system should have a personalized layout to manage multiple vendors and the products they offer. For example, your content management system should offer unique product SKUs. Additionally, you should have an automated system that quickly adds products and their data for you.

- **Offer Miscellaneous Integrations** – A content management system must have other integrated features like payment systems, email newsletters, and other services. Your platform should have multiple payment options for customers to give them flexibility in buying products from you. Compatibility can help increase your brand's reputation.

- **Features Responsive Layouts** – You will need to select a CMS that is compatible with smart devices and desktops. You want the website to open responsively on mobiles, iPads, etc., as most people use their smartphones to shop for products.

- **Supports SEO** – CMS system integrated with SEO tools can be a big boon for your dropshipping store. SEO can help optimize your business site for an authoritative presence in your target niche.

DROPSHIPPING

- **Supports Blogging** – It should also provide support for blogging if you want that to be a part of your website. When you add helpful content to your website in the form of blogs, you motivate people to purchase items from your site.

- **Costs Reasonably** – You can find content management systems available at various rates. Keep in mind your budget when choosing a CMS. Also, verify if the design templates and modules your chosen system supports are complementary or not. It all depends on how much you are willing to invest.

You will have to spend money on your dropshipping website, whether in the form of a hosting service, CMS, or other tools that you want to integrate into the system. But, fortunately, these investments may not be higher than 15% of your complete dropshipping business budget.

Which One to Choose?

You should make a choice based on the objectives you want to accomplish in your business model. If your goal is to start your business as soon as possible, choose the pre-existing platforms with hosting services and integrated CMS. But, if you want to design everything based on your own creativity, buy a domain and design/develop the website yourself, or hire professionals to do it for you. To build your brand reputation, write blogs, optimize your website with the latest SEO strategies, and build a killer marketing campaign to promote your marketplace.

DROPSHIPPING

Choosing a self-hosted service can be exciting as you will be nurturing your website like your own child. But it can take time – invest only after properly thinking it over.

Factors to Consider When Choosing a Dropshipping Platform

Now, let's look into several factors to choose a dropshipping platform:

- **Simplified Store Setup** – Choose a platform for your dropshipping business that offers help and support at every step of the process. Pay attention to the back-end operations your chosen platform can handle. After thorough research, comparing various platforms, choose the one that gives you the most features at a reasonable price.

- Customer-Friendly – Select a website that has a customer-friendly setup. Such a layout should offer an appealing homepage, ample data for customers to comprehend about your products and services, shipping and refund policy details, and a well-categorized product catalog. Choose a dropshipping platform that can offer you at least these features.

- Additionally, your products should not be misleading. For instance, think of a situation where you see an appealing product advertised on a random website. You instantly feel like clicking and buying it, but you can't find a single product resembling the one you clicked on when you get to the website. That can be frustrating, right? Avoid following such a model and

DROPSHIPPING

focus on genuinely improving the experience for your potential customer.

- You can research the dropshipping websites of your competitors to understand what a good layout should be like. After that, see if the dropshipping platform you are about to choose offers similar customizations that you find attractive.

- Supplier-Friendly – You need a dropshipping platform that can manage multiple vendors so that there is consistent availability of products for your customers. The setup should be capable of adding new products to your website within a few clicks from various suppliers' sites. Overall, you want a streamlined process to manage all your products, SKUs, and other details without mixing up vendors.

- Plugin Support – Choose a platform that gives you ample freedom to upgrade your dropshipping website. Maybe you want to add a new SEO-friendly feature to your website, or maybe you want to market your products to a new marketplace. Or perhaps you want to add a unique payment gateway like cryptocurrency. All such features should be readily available through plugins on the platform you choose.

- Customer Tracker – Every order that your website fulfills should have a proper tracking process. Find a platform that gives you the feature to streamline the operations and manage your customer and vendor data with great efficiency.

DROPSHIPPING

CHAPTER 5

MARKETING YOUR PRODUCT

Even if you have the best website, CMS, and platform for your new dropshipping business, you will still need to get customers to reach your site. To do that, your top-priority tool is going to be marketing.

To sell more, you will need a solid marketing campaign with the potential to give decent returns in the long run.

Know Your Marketing Channels

There are plenty of marketing channels available nowadays. You need to decide which one suits you best for your requirements. The ones with the most potential can give you a decent return on your investment.

You cannot simply rely on the product ideas because if you do not have a potential audience to see your products, it will all be in vain. You will need to create a solid plan on how to sell your niche products because this is significant to becoming a successful dropshipper.

DROPSHIPPING

It becomes easier to sell stuff online when you have an appropriate marketing plan. It is marketing that will help you shine among your rivals. This section will help you familiarize yourself with the various marketing channels you can choose from to create a lucrative business.

Note that some marketing platforms mentioned below will be better for selling specific products. You might not get universal results with just a single marketing channel. You will have to deduce which of them will be best suited for your dropshipping operations.

Facebook Marketing

eCommerce and Dropshipping work side by side – adding new ways of earning without the need of opening a brick-and-mortar store. It's a business model with ample opportunities to earn money online. One of the key features of the eCommerce business is that you can use your social media accounts, like Facebook, to help you make money.

Let's show you how you can do Facebook marketing for your dropshipping business.

People find it more convenient to find products they can buy at places that barely require any research work. Social media platforms like Facebook send tailor-made ads to viewers, showcasing what they might like to buy. It may sound similar to Google ads, but Facebook has the largest social network audience with numbers in the billions. Starting an advertising campaign there might not be a bad idea.

DROPSHIPPING

Unlike Google ads, which viewers have to search for, Facebook ads are much more scalable. You share the ad with a couple of customers and, from there, it reaches millions if it is in demand. Facebook ads are planned with empathy so people can relate to them and find suitable products for their use.

The key is to master creating a Facebook ad. Let's show you how you can accomplish that.

Facebook Advertising in Your Dropshipping Business

If you are aware of online marketing, you already know the importance of SEO ranking. You may also be aware that ranking a website can take time. With Facebook Ads, you can head start your marketing campaign until your organic traffic starts building up – eventually increasing your sales.

When you advertise your dropshipping business on a platform, your main objective is to generate enough traffic so that you can generate sales. You want to sell the products, for which your advertisement should be accurate enough to target potential buyers.

Facebook gives you the advantage of sharing promotional and sponsored posts in the same newsfeed. You can see the ads represented with the word "Sponsored."

How Does That Benefit You?

Your generated FB ad shows up in the newsfeed of a user's account on Facebook. Such an ad smartly blends in with the

DROPSHIPPING

other normal posts and, most of the time, the users barely notice that they are being shown a promoted post.

Psychologically, people ignore visual illustrations that are highlighted as ads, like Google ads. But, in the case of Facebook, these ads just feel like they're a normal post. If such an ad interests the user, he/she might click it and reach your website to browse for the product in the ad. Moreover, Facebook cleverly shows comments in such promoted posts, normalizing it even further to blend with the rest of the organic posts.

It's all about the first impression, which matters when selling a product successfully.

Facebook Ad Structure at a Glance

A successful Facebook Ad for a dropshipping business requires three stages:

1. *Ad Campaign (for determining the objective of the ad)*

2. *Ad sets (for categorizing the ads based on your budget and target audience)*

3. *Ads (the actual ads that viewers will see)*

Let's discuss all three.

Campaign

This stage is all about setting up the primary goals for your ad. It's the starting point when you determine how, where, and who your ads will be visible to. Let's say you have two ad sets

DROPSHIPPING

planned for your dropshipping site – one will market the complete website, and the other markets various deals on particular products.

With ad objectives in your campaign, you are generally accomplishing the following objectives:

- Increase traffic to the website as much as possible
- Accomplish more likes on your posts and Facebook page
- Maximize your business audience
- Feature offers from time to time
- Boost brand awareness
- Increase the sales of individual products listed on your dropshipping website.

When creating a campaign, you will have to categorize every ad carefully based on your objectives. You will also want to create an appropriate "campaign" for every category of products.

Ad Sets

In this phase, you are organizing the ads based on your target audience. You will categorize the audience based on their personal interests, purchasing frequency, recent events in their lives, their commenting and liking activities on various posts, their joined Facebook groups, occupation, and demography.

DROPSHIPPING

If you like, you can use "Facebook Audience Insights," which is a Facebook tool for helping you organize the process easily. It comes with the Facebook Ads Manager account.

For instance, if your niche products for sale are sports accessories, you will add details to your ad set for a 'personalized audience.' You will specify another ad set for individuals in the local area. You may also add another set targeting people who have made a purchase from your site in the past.

Ads

In this stage, you use organized ad sets and relevant data to your targeted audiences for marketing purposes. You create an actual ad in this phase that will be seen by the viewers from around the targeted demography. You will create several images, descriptions, and logos for every ad set you generate to see what works effectively for the masses.

Marketers often run ads using A/B tests, which means you create multiple ads with little changes made to each. You never know which ad may help you boost the conversion rate.

Targeting the Right People

It's a very simple logic: match ads with products that people find interesting or that are meant for them in a way.

You would not target your ads showcasing Mothercare products to a guy, would you?

DROPSHIPPING

Studies show that much dropshipping business fails considerably because the ads are not targeted toward the right masses. On the contrary, many businesses flourished because their ads reached the right viewers, who converted to customers eventually. So, you have to be careful when choosing the audience for your ads. If you have done ample research on your dropshipping niche, you will find it much easier to plan your potential audience.

Occupation, Interest, and Demography

It's quite obvious – a high school girl will not browse for the same items from your dropshipping website as a 70-year-old man. To make it easier, "Facebook Audience Insight" will be a helpful tool to allow you to organize your primarily targeted audience by their:

- Occupation
- Age
- Interests (Facebook groups they have joined, pages they comment on, posts they like)
- Hobbies
- Purchasing Frequency
- Recent life events

If your niche products include cutlery, Facebook will autonomously filter out the users who recently purchased products related to the kitchen or anything related to that or

DROPSHIPPING

who have had an interest in browsing them or are a part of a group in that niche.

It's like a laser targeting system that helps you look for potential customers without too much manual work. That's what you need for your dropshipping marketplace.

Geography

Focusing on geography in your ad campaign is important so that you can narrow down the area of the target. The more concentrated your target circle is, the faster you will succeed at converting leads. The location should be one of the key preferences that will help you strengthen your Facebook Ad model for your dropshipping business. A potential customer located in a snowy region may find little use for an above-ground swimming pool. It is important that you target potential buyers within a specific geographical circle where you believe your products can reach them most effectively.

Custom Audiences

With Facebook marketing tools, you can create your personalized audience list to target your products. Creating a viewers' list will make it easier to find the right prospects with a high probability of buying your products. Such lists can feature past clients, individuals who contacted you personally about a particular product, or people who reviewed your products positively. You can even target them with special offers or giveaways through Facebook Messenger.

Planning the Budget

DROPSHIPPING

Whether the amount is little or not, it matters when you spend it. In a dropshipping business, every penny is worth spending in the right way. To make sure that you do not waste your resources, we recommend planning everything slowly and smartly. Instead of spending it all at once, invest a small portion of it and see how your ad campaigns work.

Analyze your growth after the first investment and make financial decisions accordingly. Using "Facebook Advertising Tool," you have the advantage of paying for the ads daily or in a lump-sum, which is called the "Lifetime Budget." It depends on you how you want to proceed with the money you have for investing.

Make sure you are testing out new ways of improving your ads. You may lose money on a new technique, but you will not lose all of your money if you invest smartly. On the bright side, you will know that a failed ad has something wrong with it, which you can change and try again.

Learn the lessons from your creative ads and focus on the marketing part. Remember that this is the only main operation you have to do in a dropshipping business because the inventory management, picking, packaging, and shipping part will be the responsibility of your third-party supplier. Find new and effective ways to market your products so that you can get potential customers to boost your business.

Choose your ad campaign budget and utilize the money in the right direction with experience. Facebook will spend your invested money in two ways: based on the CPC (Cost Per Clicks) or CPM (Cost Per 1000 Impressions). With CPC,

DROPSHIPPING

Facebook will generate ads on its own for you with the most relevant data to your product niche. With CPM, it will deduct money whenever your ad reaches 1000 impressions.

Facebook Ads Placement For Dropshipping

You are provided with five choices to place your ads on Facebook. These are:

- Desktop Feed
- Mobile Feed
- Instagram Feed
- Audience Network
- Right Column Feed (Desktop)

As per previous data, Mobile feed and Desktop feed are the most popular and have been known to produce the most traffic. You don't have to place ads in all of these, like the Right Column feed for desktops, which users ignore the most because it resembles an ad that online users are used to seeing on Google, etc.

Key Points to Include in a Facebook Ad

A successful Facebook ad should:

- Target potential customers who are willing to buy something based on the various categories.

DROPSHIPPING

- Build communication with your website viewers through email newsletters.

- Include a call-to-action to lead customers to your website.

- Not focus on the sales point of view directly.

- Offer giveaways and offers to your viewers.

- Utilize Facebook's carousel feature.

- Feature a price point.

- Share high-quality images and videos to build an audience.

- Focus on segmenting a well-targeted audience.

Summarizing the Steps to Set Up Facebook Ads to Improve Dropshipping Sales

Investing in Facebook ads can do wonders for your business. To do that, you will need to set up a proper marketing campaign on this popular social media platform.

Here are the general steps you should follow:

1. Set Up Facebook Pixel

Facebook Pixel can give you a head start in your social media marketing campaign. It is an analyzing tool that lets you know how well your ads are performing on your website. Pixel lets you target your ads to the right people. You can go to the ads

DROPSHIPPING

manager section of Facebook to "Create a Pixel" if you want to do it manually. Either way, Facebook can generate it automatically for you. Paste the generated pixel code on the webpages you want to analyze and let Facebook do its magic.

2. Create an Ad Account

To start making Facebook ads, you will first need to set up an ad account. With this account, you will make people aware of your brand and reach out to them even more. You will need to set up the Facebook Ads Manager to start with the marketing campaign. Furthermore, you will set up a target audience based on demographics and geographic area. You can optimize your ads here, noting the impressions, setting a target budget, etc.

3. Monitor Ads

You cannot just create ads and leave them be. You also have to analyze their performance to ensure a successful campaign. Take note of significant factors, such as Cost Per Action (CPA). Pay close attention to such features and make sure that their value is as high as possible so Facebook can optimize your campaigns gradually. Another factor to keep track of is the Click Through Rate (CTR). If this value goes down, it means your ads are not being watched. This number also needs to be high, so you will know your ads are getting views. A low CTR suggests that something is not right about the ad. You may need to make a few changes and analyze them again.

4. Optimize Ad Campaigns

DROPSHIPPING

As mentioned earlier, your work is not limited to creating ads and analyzing them. You will have to optimize them from time to time so that they show up as better numbers. It can be time-consuming at first, but you get better at this with time. Eventually, you will get perfect at deducing the right geographic areas and age groups to target with your ad campaigns.

Etsy Marketing

Dropshippers are always looking for new and efficient ways to market trending products and search for new products from various online stores, and Etsy is one of them. It's not your usual marketplace to dropship.

It's a place where you will find buyers investing in quirky products popular among the younger generation. With over 2.1 million vendors and over 40 million buyers listed on Etsy, you can consider this online platform to give you a lucrative market to promote your products.

Despite being a household name, Etsy's marketing for dropshipping is not for everyone. In this chapter, you will learn about Etsy, its pros and cons, and understand how you can market your products using this marketplace.

What is Etsy?

Etsy is a powerful eCommerce platform with a global reach. It usually engages in the trading of customized products. Etsy is one of the chief platforms to promote the growth of small businesses that want to sell their products.

DROPSHIPPING

This marketplace was established in 2005, and it has since generated over $200 million in revenue by the end of 2019. Despite the high number of buyers on this platform, many consumers and business owners underestimate this platform. But Etsy has potential that, if mastered, can result in really high returns in the long run.

Etsy navigation for dropshippers requires a little creativity with crafty entrepreneurship. You need to work hard to understand what is trending on the market to create a loyal client base that is ready to invest in your promoted products for the long term.

The Main Techniques of Etsy Dropshipping

Many dropshippers feel skeptical about using Etsy because it does not follow a beaten track. But that's the good thing about it. If you can avoid a majority of the competition, you can create a reliable eCommerce store for marketing your products.

Etsy uses two techniques for dropshipping:

The first one involves using another vendor's Etsy storefront as your own dropshipping store. But there is a limit to it. Etsy will not let you dropship other Etsy seller's products if they are handcrafted by him/her. Etsy considers dropshipping of handcrafted products illegal. So, you might not have a direct way of reselling such products.

Instead, you can create a storefront outside Etsy and sell the vintage and crafted goods from there.

DROPSHIPPING

The other method involves opening an Etsy storefront yourself and dropship from non-Etsy manufacturers. You can get the products from such non-Etsy stores and outsource them with your design to make them look like your handcrafted products.

These methods may seem complicated, but they are the best you can use if you plan to use Etsy marketing for your dropshipping business. This brings us to the section where we discuss the advantages and disadvantages of using dropshipping from Etsy.

The Pros & Cons of Etsy Dropshipping

The Pros

- **Patient and Conscious Buyers**

If you choose to open an Etsy storefront, you can sell directly to Etsy buyers. Since its existence, this marketplace has garnered a unique and loyal community of consumers and manufacturers that desire uniqueness, human-centric goods, and craftsmanship. With such encompassing core values, being a part of such a platform can be quite beneficial in a way.

Etsy buyers know that high-quality handcrafted goods can take time to produce and for shipment. And such individuals are ready to spend more to buy a premium-quality product. That can be a beneficial point for your dropshipping business. Unlike other eCommerce stores, you can create patient and loyal customers if you have the right goods to suit their tastes.

- **Room for Creativity**

DROPSHIPPING

In Etsy dropshipping, businessmen will never run out of creative ideas because they do not need to tend to other operations like logistics, packaging, and production. Etsy is perfect for the ones who want to actively participate in designing without the need for manufacturing or handling shipment. One such way to invest your creativity on this platform is through Etsy Umbrella, which lets entrepreneurs craft their brand in creative ways.

- **Creation of a Unique Product Inventory**

Dropshipping is an uncontrolled process in the world of eCommerce, and it tends to get more challenging for entrepreneurs from all over the globe. However, Etsy has an intuitive way of handling common goods by providing buyers with one-of-a-kind and original products. You can stock such products and make a living out of this business if you have the right products to outsource to your potential consumers.

- **Potential Platform for Niche Products**

We have mentioned earlier too that dropshipping is quite successful if you target niche products. And Etsy is the perfect place to market such products. You can choose from one of many thriving product industries, such as baby goods, clothing, home products, and wedding products, to create a loyal customer base.

Etsy is the best sorted out place for niche goods, which is why both customers and makers flock to this eCommerce site to trade in a specific item they like. This portal has worked hard to build a reputation that provides specialty and unusual items

DROPSHIPPING

fit for buyers. And it does so without making you work extra hard.

- **Decent Profits**

If you have been surfing around Etsy's product listings, you will notice the high retail costs on most of the products. Without a doubt, many goods listed there are quite high in price compared to their market value. But sellers do not have to worry about closing the deals there because of the loyal customers. Buyers are ready to buy products from this website because of the reputation Etsy has built up for its products catalog.

For dropshippers, this can have a lot of potential considering the profits. They can rely on loyal customers that know Etsy's reputation, which is why they are willing to pay extra for quality. Some dropshippers can even get a 40% profit margin or even more.

- **Transparency**

Transparency in a business can help customers know that you are an authentic vendor ready to deliver quality products to them. So, they are more willing to spend their money to buy goods from you. Moreover, Etsy obligates sellers to disclose their business location. This level of transparency and honesty has made Etsy a successful platform for buyers and sellers.

Customers have a sense of relief knowing that they will not be trapped in the crooked world of eCommerce, where sellers often indulge in selling and reselling activities to earn a profit.

DROPSHIPPING

Buyers who are willing to spend money on these products, want to know where they are being produced. This transparency is even more necessary in the online world.

Etsy requires members to provide a valid business location where the handmade goods are being made, supporting firsthand manufacturers. So, you will need to mold your dropshipping business plan to resell goods in such a way that they look like your brand's handmade products.

The Cons

While Etsy dropshipping has many benefits, it also has limitations, and you must know about them too before investing in this marketing model.

Let's take a look:

- **High Fees**

Just like other eCommerce retail platforms, Etsy also adds fees on selling products. When you open a dropshipping storefront Etsy, you have to be aware of a few types of fees. For example, there is a listing fee of $0.20 on products. This listing expires after every four months.

This fee may look like a minute amount, but it can affect your profit margins at times. If you set this listing fee for automatic renewal, your account will automatically be deducted with the fees after every four months whenever your list expires. If you choose to update to a manual renewal setting, you will have to invest your time and effort in updating your list every four months.

DROPSHIPPING

Another problem is that Etsy charges you a processing fee of 5% on every product you sell. On top of that, this fee does not even include the shipping charges. No doubt Etsy has been known for maintaining quality for its buyers and sellers, but that comes at a price. Its resources and add-on tools for sellers, with in-person fees, pattern fees, ad fees, etc., all sum up to a hefty sum that sellers have to pay to be a part of this platform.

- **Severe Guidelines for Dropshipping Models**

By now, you are already aware of Etsy's intense business model. Their rules are quite strict, making sure every interaction, transaction, and process among sellers and buyers go through their codes of conduct for supplying handmade goods. The dense and extensive eCommerce model works to make sure that dropshipping of handmade products stay off their platform.

Etsy allows sellers to resell craft supplies and vintage goods. Furthermore, the retail store allows sellers to assist manufacturers that produce unique designs but are not good at marketing their products. According to Etsy, some businesses manufacture original products with their tools and hands in-house, and others may not have the skills and means to create such products on their own but have the skills to sell them. This platform allows both types of sellers to carry out their business without problems.

Certainly, there are specific rules and regulations behind how such products should be sold on the platform. For instance, sharing the location where the products are being

DROPSHIPPING

manufactured is a must, and not all dropshipping businesses are ready to do that.

- **Severe Community Policies for Sellers**

Etsy wants its portal to run uniformly and fairly for the traders. To do that, it has various policies that sellers have to follow strictly. Otherwise, the platform may penalize you with fees, etc.

Additionally, Etsy monitors transaction activities for the allowed third-party payment gateways. For instance, it will keep an eye on the accounts and transactions made via payment portals like PayPal so that you do not violate any of their policies in the process.

On top of that, Etsy has an extensive way of scrutinizing dropshipping businesses on its platform. While its support for original makers and their storefronts is appealing with decent profit margins, dropshippers and resellers have a lot to sacrifice to survive there.

- **Operations Based on Trade Restrictions and Economic Sanctions**

Here is a simple explanation for this con: Etsy is a worldwide online eCommerce store, but its primary base is in the U.S. That means it has to follow the economic sanctions and government policies of that country. As a result, not everyone has access to this platform. Several geographic regions cannot use Etsy. Moreover, you cannot resell products made in those restricted places. You need to be cautious about where your

DROPSHIPPING

products originally come from because that can impact your profit margins and sales.

- **Exhausting Listing Process**

Etsy has a very tedious process for listing products on the website. One of the main reasons is that this online portal is more inclined toward small manufacturers and handmade products, which have many variations. For consumers, Etsy tries to create an in-depth portal consisting of information telling customers about every product they might like to buy.

But that leads to a lot of work for the sellers because they have to fill in most of the details to make sure that their products are genuine with high-quality features. Specifying all the details for the buyers on this platform can take time and effort.

How to Dropship Products From Etsy

Despite the cons, many dropshippers have a keen eye on grabbing the Etsy customer base by selling products in various ways. The model might not be straightforward for a dropshipping business model, but it is worth it to get high-profit margins if you know how to do it. You need proper relationships and channels readily at your disposal to successfully master this platform.

Here's a simple way of uploading products from Etsy to another e-store. In this step, we will take Shopify as the other platform for your storefront.

DROPSHIPPING

- Research. You need to first look for manufacturers and sellers on Etsy that match your mission and brand requirements.

- Have a clear agreement. Communicate with potential sellers on the platform and clarify all the details of the dropshipping business deal with them.

- Add a Shopify extension. You need to use the Chrome browser to find this extension and install it.

- Use the extension to list Etsy products. To achieve this step, go to the Etsy platform and go on the product page. Click the extension button, which will prompt you to add all the relevant details. For the product description section, make sure the wording varies.

These steps should list the Etsy product on your Shopify storefront.

On the other hand, if you want to open an Etsy storefront, you can easily create a page on the Etsy website. But you will need to:

- Have original products ready for your store or search for a manufacturing partner for potential products.

- Calculate all the fees, profit margins, and prices.

- Register your business on Etsy through their online portal. To do that, you will need to provide a name for your storefront, payment methods, billing details, product partner's information, and the list of products.

DROPSHIPPING

From here, you are responsible for coming up with a killer marketing campaign to promote the products you want to resell.

Once you have done all these steps, you are ready to start your dropshipping business via Etsy. If everything is fine, you will have a business model that only focuses on promoting products, leaving the manufacturing and shipping part to your third-party supplier.

Etsy FAQs for Dropshipping

A lot of people might have queries about dropshipping through Etsy. We have answered a few of those frequently asked questions so you can have a clear idea of this business model.

Is It Legal to Dropship With Etsy?

The answer is complicated. The dropshipping business model for this platform is not straightforward. For instance, you will have to develop a clear agreement with a seller who will ship the sold products to your customers.

Additionally, you have many restrictions on reselling various products in this marketplace. If you do not have any involvement in producing handmade products, you cannot sell them there. You will only be left with options like vintage and handmade crafts. Plus, you will need to disclose your location where the production of goods you are reselling occurs. If you fail to follow Etsy's rules, the site can penalize you or even ban your account.

DROPSHIPPING

How to Search for a Potential Manufacturing Partner for Your Etsy Dropshipping Business

Keeping in mind that Etsy prohibits outsourcing products that sellers do not manufacture, you have limited choices to find sellers on the platform itself –or at least the ones who can supply handmade goods to your customers.

A feasible option is to find manufacturers who are outside of Etsy. You can look for small businesses that are still strangers to online marketplaces and help them earn a share by promoting their products through an Etsy storefront.

If you are keen on searching for a seller through Etsy only, you can come up with an agreement with that vendor by working together. That way, Etsy will not have a problem as long as you are seen as a partner with the manufacturer's business.

To do that, you can search for various sellers on the platform and contact them with your proposal. That's the best and the most straightforward way to achieve your dropshipping goals.

Is Etsy for You?

Etsy's marketplace is not meant for everyone, but you can enjoy its highly lucrative profit margins if you manage to fulfill its eligibility criteria. It is a great way to improve your dropshipping business only when you have the right resources supporting you.

To survive here, you will need to plan your goals for the business and brand strategically. Your role in this business model requires active participation to stay up to date with the

DROPSHIPPING

product listings, promotions, and policies. But most dropshippers may not want to have an extensive business model like this. For them, other marketing strategies could work better.

Amazon Marketing

Dropshipping beginners often look for the eCommerce stores that they are most familiar with, and Amazon is certainly one of the first options that come to mind. After all, it's the most popular shopping platform in the U.S., with 150+ million users on its mobile platform in September 2019.

Moreover, Amazon is a trusted brand with strong customer loyalty. Selling to people in such a huge virtual marketplace can be rewarding. Amazon can offer you a smoother experience compared to Etsy or Facebook when it comes to dropshipping. But you do need to understand the basic process and the rules related to it.

This section will look into the dropshipping process on Amazon and explain how to sell on this platform, the benefits of dropshipping on this portal, and give you helpful tools for Amazon dropshipping.

Let's get started.

How Does Dropshipping Work on Amazon?

Amazon provides a dedicated feature to dropship bought items to customers. Using it, Amazon handles the inventory and shipment of your products, sending them directly to your consumers.

DROPSHIPPING

Amazon provides a fast and reliable shipping process, which can be beneficial for your dropshipping business. Customers feel more inclined to choose services that offer fast deliveries.

Let's explain the benefits you can get through the largest eCommerce portal in the world.

Amazon Dropshipping Benefits

- **Negligible Warehouse Expenses**

Amazon has one of the largest shipping and handling programs, with millions of products shipped daily. This means you do not have to pay warehouse costs. The company's FBA (Fulfilled by Amazon) program helps sellers streamline their product handling. With FBA, sellers can send an ordered product to the Amazon warehouse, and Amazon then ships it to your customer.

- **Amazon Suppliers**

Amazon has to ship products daily, so it buys hundreds and thousands of products in bulk from various suppliers and stores them in its warehouses. These products are ready to ship to customers at short notice. Furthermore, it takes care of the customer service and returned items in various languages for all its suppliers.

As a dropshipper, you can partner with Amazon as your supplier, which will take care of all the product handling and shipping for you. And it is worth mentioning Amazon also appoints account managers who are willing to help small

DROPSHIPPING

businesses, sellers, and resellers all the time to increase profits for all parties.

- **Large Customer Base**

One of the most profitable businesses in the world surely has one of the largest customer bases. With over 300 million active consumers, Amazon is a vast channel for your business, supporting your growth. Selling the products with potential at the right price can help you create a list of loyal customers.

Furthermore, the platform is visited by millions of people daily. Starting a new dropshipping storefront on an unknown or new website would require a lot of time and effort to lure customers. Amazon gives that to you from the start, which saves a lot of time.

- **Diversified Categories with Potential**

Amazon has 30+ product categories, which can help you choose various niche products you wish to resell. Choosing the right products and reliable vendors can help boost your brand presence, as more and more customers come willingly to buy from your storefront.

How to Sell on Amazon

- **Select a Potential eCommerce Portal**

You will need an eCommerce platform with the potential to sell relevant products. A good option is to choose Shopify, which is an Amazon-partner. Using it would be an ideal option

DROPSHIPPING

to start your dropshipping business because Shopify lets sellers manage orders on both platforms simultaneously.

- **Choose Your Niche Products**

Amazon has various restrictions and requirements for store owners who want to sell their items there. Amazon allows you to open a store without any need for approval as per the list of eligible stores on the platform. To do that, you will need to sell in a niche such as office products, computer & video games, books, and similar products.

You should make sure to check out Amazon's restricted product list so you do not violate their rules and lose a potential business.

- **Create Your Seller Account**

If you want to dropship products in high volume, it's ideal that you create a professional seller account on the online store. Using an individual seller account will cost you 0.99 cents per sold product, which can be hard on your profits.

It is also worth mentioning that you might not be the only seller with the product on the eCommerce platform, so your prices need to be competitive with appealing discounts from time to time. You will have to make sure all this is possible while maintaining a decent profit margin for yourself so that you can reinvest in your dropshipping business and aim for more.

That's why opening a professional account where you pay a monthly subscription fee will be much easier to handle than

DROPSHIPPING

the basic seller's account protocols. To register, you will need to input your details like email, name, and password on Amazon Seller Central. You will also add further details related to your business, address, and tax info.

- **Get Approval for Your Product Category**

Amazon needs to approve specific product types and niches. Some popular ones are jewelry, beauty, and fashion niche products. You can find the latest approval requirements for all such categories on Amazon.

- **Link Your Amazon account With Shopify**

After getting approval for your Amazon seller account, you need to connect it to your Shopify store, which is highly recommended, as mentioned previously. In your Shopify account, go to the left panel, find the 'Sales Channel' button, and click it.

A pop-up should show up that highlights Amazon as one of the options. Click the 'Add Channel' button to add and press 'Connect to Amazon.'

- **Generate Amazon Product Listings**

Click the link highlighting the Amazon sales channel. To do that, you need to view the left panel on Shopify. Click on the 'Create Listing' button.

After that, click the "Select Product" button. You'll find two options there. If you have manufacturing rights to the products you want to sell, you'll have to buy UPCs. Since you are opening a dropshipping business, you are opening the account to resell products, so you'll choose the other option stating, "This product is made by another brand."

Next, search for the product to find potential sellers for relevant SKUs. Select the product that you want to list by clicking 'Select.' Then, click 'Publish' once you have listed all processes to complete the process.

- **Allow Shopify for Tracking Inventory**

You must enable this option so that Shopify can track your inventory because that will help the system to recognize if the product a customer is searching for is still available or not.

Keep a check on the accounts so that you don't let customers buy products that are unavailable in your stock. That can affect your brand's reputation, leading to negative reviews and more time on customer services.

- **Promote Your Amazon Storefront**

You certainly need to market your listed products, don't you? This step involves luring customers.

Use social media sites to spread the word for your listed products. You will have to target the right folks so they can come to visit your marketplace and buy items from you.

DROPSHIPPING

Strategies for a Successful Amazon Dropshipping Store

In this section of dropshipping with Amazon guide, you'll learn interesting strategies for a successful Amazon dropshipping business model.

- **Focus on the Amazon Buy Box**

The Amazon Buy Box has great selling potential. As a dropshipper, you need to have the Buy Box, which will showcase your listed product among all other seller products directly to customers. And that can help you boost your sales for good.

Your first step to achieve that is to improve your seller rating. Many sellers have improved their chances of getting the Buy Box with at least a 95% rating.

The next step is to make sure that your products ship quickly, within a period of 14 days.

The final step is to make sure your product and shipping costs are lower than those of your competition. A great feedback score, fast client-response time, and low refund rate can be additional factors to help you acquire the Buy Box.

- • Do Not Depend Solely on Amazon

Amazon might have a lot of resources to help you sell, but that does not mean you should rely on them for all your product sales. You will need to explore other potential platforms as well. Amazon is just one of the several sales channels that can

DROPSHIPPING

help you increase your odds of better sales with minimum risks.

Shopify will let you add more sales channels, like Facebook Marketplace, Instagram, and Messenger, to help you lure more customers.

If a customer familiarizes themselves with your brand, he/she will buy from your store on Amazon no matter where your brand exists.

- **Aim for a High Seller Rating**

A high seller rating can improve your dropshipping store in several ways. As mentioned earlier, you will also have a higher probability of getting that Buy Box. That way, you will be more visible to the customers when they are organically searching for products that you have.

Plus, a high rating offers a significant boost to earn the trust of your customer. It ensures Amazon that your storefront has potential, so it will highlight your listed products to the user more often.

- **Focus on Keyword Research**

Optimizing your Amazon product pages can help you get organic traffic, who may end up buying products from your store frequently. You can use specific keywords that can help with the SEO of your product listing pages.

DROPSHIPPING

Tools such as Merchant Words can be helpful to find keywords. Running Amazon ads can get you access to decent keywords to add to your product pages and optimize them.

It is a strategy that you should practice and master because it will help you rank higher among your rivals. When you run ads, you have a higher chance of targeting your customers effectively.

- **Set Product Prices Accordingly**

You need to keep in mind certain factors when setting prices for products on Amazon. You also want to keep track of the Amazon fee structure, which is monthly for a professional seller account. Calculating all the expenses will help you decide the right profit margin for selling the products.

- **Offer Discounts**

Sellers often give discounts to their customers through Amazon coupons. As a new dropshipper on Amazon, you will have to provide a competitive discount price to encourage buyers to check your products. You can create Amazon coupons and use other platforms to promote the codes, which can drive traffic to your storefront. But make sure you decide on a discount price without affecting your profit margin.

- **Optimize the Product Titles**

Amazon has been partial toward product titles that are relevant to customer's searches. And it makes sense – after all, stuffing keywords in the title without any planning is only going to be counterproductive.

DROPSHIPPING

Using titles that target the intent of the customers can get more attention from them. You should do a little brainstorming and develop product titles relevant to the user searches to find products.

Important attributes that should be a part of the title include quantity, color, size, model, etc. Additionally, you should always start with the brand name, which can help customers recognize your storefront for future buys if they like your product.

Amazon Dropshipping Tools

Now, let's explain some tools that you can use when starting Amazon dropshipping.

- **Merchant Words**

As stated earlier, Merchant Word is a worthy tool that can help you find data and volume on potential keywords. Its professional plan will cost you about $30 per month.

- **FeedCheck**

This tool lets you view all the customer feedback on your products in one spot. It's ideal for those sellers who have to deal with a lot of Amazon products. By staying up to date with the product reviews, you can improve your performance, aiming for better customer service. Also, you can use this tool to check your rival's products. Its plan starts at $19 per month.

- **Shopify**

DROPSHIPPING

We already discussed so much about Shopify before, stating its unlimited potential to help you create a lucrative dropshipping model with Amazon. Furthermore, Shopify can also keep track of your inventory and alert you about any Amazon sales that need fulfillment.

- **Sellery**

This tool offers various tactics so you can get the Amazon Buy Box. It lets you fiddle with the product pricing so you can stay ahead of your competition and boost your profits. Luckily, this tool is free to use.

- **Feedback Express**

This tool assists you with getting additional customer feedback on your store. It also helps manage the negative reviews so that you maintain a high rating on your niche store and products. Feedback Express even lets you blacklist customers who keep spamming by leaving negative reviews. Its price plan starts at $20 per month.

- **Amazon Volume Listing Spreadsheets**

Amazon features a bunch of tools to help sellers have a streamlined experience. Sellers can download spreadsheets that can help manage inventory and orders with other detailed information. You can use these tools to modify product quantity and pricing with ease.

DROPSHIPPING

Dropshipping From Amazon to eBay

Another popular dropshipping model besides Shopify is eBay. This process involves sellers buying products at a lower price from Amazon and selling them for a profit on eBay. This business model has been going on for many years now.

In this model, the end customer, who purchases a product from eBay, will receive the item with Amazon packing. The end-user receives the product; the overall experience is not that great at times.

Technically, this method is not illegal, but manufacturers don't like this way of doing business. That's because dropshippers benefit from it without the manufacturer even knowing about it.

eBay also does not want to partake in such a model, which is why in 2017, it banned hundreds of vendors from Israel who used dropshipping.

That's one reason why your dropshipping business needs to be highly reputed. It should avoid practicing malicious techniques that will only hinder your brand reputation.

Pinterest Marketing

Many are not even aware that Pinterest can be an excellent tool for eCommerce use, even for dropshipping. That's one reason why you can explore this side of the marketing strategy for your dropshipping model to boost new opportunities for sales without incurring additional expenses.

DROPSHIPPING

In this section, we'll look at ways to use Pinterest for dropshipping so you can increase the potential of your business.

What is Pinterest?

Like Instagram and Facebook, Pinterest is a social media portal that lets users share visual images (individually or collectively) related to things that they like or that are trending. Similar to other popular social media platforms, you can generate followers on Pinterest as well. You can even share links to content related to other social media pages, websites, blogs, etc.

It has features such as Pinterest Gifts and Rich Pins, which let users improve their CTR, helping with better conversions for dropshipping storefronts, etc.

The site also has Buyable pins, which people can use to buy products directly from the platform. That makes shopping quite convenient and easily accessible for end customers.

<u>Why is Pinterest Marketing Profitable for Dropshipping Business?</u>

Dropshippers who are still not on Pinterest might be missing a gold mine. There are so many uncharted opportunities on this portal that can help increase the productivity and revenue of your business without the need for extra investment.

Let's give you a few reasons to try Pinterest out.

- **Vast Community**

DROPSHIPPING

Like other popular social media platforms, Pinterest also has over 200 million active users, among whom about 60% are females, and 40% are males. The numbers have been increasing ever since its start as more and more entrepreneurs realize the benefits of using Pinterest for their online stores.

- **Decent Usage**

Many users access the Pinterest app for an average of 15 minutes per session, surfing for things they like or just finding something interesting. That time which they give to the platform is an opportunity that can let you lure customers to your web store.

- **Opportunistic**

With more and more people already using it, why shouldn't you? Two-thirds of the Pins present on Pinterest are from business websites. Big and small brands all use it to compete and get as many customers as they can. Moreover, your potential customers are also using it, making it a good place to promote your niche products.

- **High Visibility**

You use pins to share your posts on Pinterest. When a customer sees and likes your product post, he/she clicks on the pin, which takes the user directly to the main source. That's an intriguing way to increase traffic to your store. This effective feature makes Pinterest quite popular among businesses.

- **Better Engagement**

DROPSHIPPING

Pinterest offers you the opportunity to have a better engagement session with your present customers. You can easily use the platform to understand what they like, which can be helpful when selecting the right products for them.

- **Optimized**

A Pinterest account showing your products can have better organic growth, making your dropshipping storefront gather better Google rankings.

- **Improved Brand Reputation**

Pinterest is known to share creative products, which can well support improving your brand's reputation. You can create Pinterest boards highlighting products to increase your brand identity. Pinterest lets you create a display window, showing off various items of interest to your potential customers.

- **Longevity**

Unlike Facebook, Twitter, or Instagram, the content on Pinterest stays there forever. People search for products or posts related to the items you sell, and when they find them – they re-pin them so others can see them too. That way, interesting content never fades away on this platform.

- **Inspiring**

All types of users visit Pinterest for inspiration related to new products, creativity, and other interests. As a dropshipper, you can share your niche products with users, who might find the items worth checking out – possibly, buying too.

DROPSHIPPING

- **Free of Charge**

When you are getting a marketing platform free of cost, you should grab it. Pinterest gives you that opportunity to use the platform as freely as you like. That means your brand can improve its organic reach without the need to spend any money.

Now, let's learn how you can use Pinterest for your dropshipping web store.

How to Use Pinterest for Dropshipping Business

1. Start by Setting Up Your Business Account

If you want to use all the featured tools like Pins, Analytics, and more on Pinterest, you have to create a business account. Start by selecting a name for your account.

While choosing a name, keep in mind the following:

- Use a relevant business name or something similar to your dropshipping business. That way, users will find you easily on other social media platforms as well.

- Choose a relevant business profile picture. An ideal choice would be to upload your brand logo.

- Write a clear description of your business. This description needs to be concise, as you will only get 160 characters to tell readers about your business. Make sure it is appealing and unique to the viewers so they can check out what you have for them.

DROPSHIPPING

- Remember to mention your website URL so people can find your original platform or website.

2. Integrate Pinterest with Social Media Platforms

After setting up the business account with all the relevant dropshipping business details, you need to let the crowd know of your presence on Pinterest. To do that, you can integrate Pinterest with your social media accounts, blog, and online store. That's who you can make your business influential and dominant in the eCommerce industry.

A resourceful way to do this is by using Pinterest's Widget Builder. With this tool, you can link your store utilizing the various options available there. You can add widgets and buttons to your web store quite easily. A few of them are mentioned below:

- **Save Button** - lets users save what they find interest on your website.

- **Follow Button** - lets users follow you on Pinterest.

- **Pin Widget** - can be embedded with a link to your blog or online store, helping you drive organic traffic to your Pinterest account or website.

- **Profile Widget** - lets you show up to 30 pins present on your Pinterest account on the dropshipping storefront.

- **Board Widget** - shows the latest pins (up to 30) from your boards of interest on Pinterest.

DROPSHIPPING

3. Optimize Your Dropshipping Webstore with Pinterest

After integrating your Pinterest account with other social media and web platforms related to your dropshipping store, it's time to optimize it. You can do this by adding images and content to your Pinterest account so users can be directed there and vice versa.

You can also embed Pinterest images on your blog site to create fresh and relevant content. That way, users can pin content that they like, which will also be searchable on Pinterest, helping you get more visibility.

You have to make sure that the images you embed or use are unique and high-quality, so they instantly attract the users' attention. That will also trigger them to pin the content.

4. Content Optimization

Pinterest is an ideal platform for users who want to search for things of interest, brands, products, and ideas. To stand out from the crowd, make sure your content catches the eye of the viewer instantly. Your content should be sufficiently intriguing that users feel excited to go through all your posts.

You can start by installing the Pin button so you can collect relevant images to display on your Pinterest portal. Your followers will see and like those images. Remember that your content should not just be related to your niche products. Collect and pin visual images that people find useful, informative, and fascinating.

DROPSHIPPING

For example, if you own a car accessories store, you can add content related to renovating a car's interior and pin it on your webstore. Furthermore, you can add quotes from celebrities related to the automotive world. It's all about engaging the users so they can interact with your store as often as possible.

Visual information has so much more to say than words, which is why you need to choose attractive images to motivate your followers to perform an action, like repinning your embedded image, making a purchase, or clicking the link.

Choose various sources so that you can collect unique images to share with your followers, making things interesting all the time.

5. Create Customized Images for Your Dropshipping Store

When you share unique images on your portal, you are organically optimizing your web authority, prompting search engines like Google to boost visibility to your dropshipping store.

So, instead of sharing existing images, why not create personalized images to ensure uniqueness? To do that, you can use pre-designed templates on Pinterest and give them your personal touch. One way to do it by using picture-editing tools like Canva. You can use its free version or buy the professional version to start creating beautiful and inspiring images for your account on Pinterest.

After that, make sure you write a killer description for the created images. Pins that have images with descriptions have a higher probability of being shared or re-pinned. Write intriguing and exciting descriptions for the images. And add the URL to your website wherever you feel is relevant.

6. Engage Your Viewers With Pinterest Boards

You can also use Pinterest Boards, which are an effective way to promote your products and engage the audience. You can create several boards on the platform. However, you should make sure that each board represents a particular niche or topic related to your business or interests.

For instance, if you have a store related to kitchen knives, you can create a Pinterest board sharing images and videos related to knives used by famous chefs. That would be quite interesting, wouldn't it?

Emphasize the name and description for your board. Once the board is re-pinned, your board's name and description are also reposted, which can be a great way to promote your dropshipping store. Create interesting descriptions that grab the user's attention so they feel an urge to visit your online store.

Here are some things that you can do with a Pinterest board:

- Send an invitation to your followers to add them to your board or create a board for them and their interests and share it with yourself. These ways are great to engage and interact with the audience. You can also get new ideas when you communicate with them, giving you more ways to be creative.

DROPSHIPPING

- Create content on your boards to sell products related to your brand and lifestyle choices. Help people who are finding new and interesting things on Pinterest so that they instantly feel inspired seeing your content.

- For example, if your dropship business is related to camping essentials and gear, you can create a board that shares a 'weekend camping trip essentials' or 'safety tips while camping solo.' Such content will be interesting for viewers who love to camp or are planning to camp.

- You can also create giveaway contests to lure more traffic to your account on Pinterest. Creating a board that specifically shares giveaway campaigns can be a great way to improve your following.

- Do not forget to use hashtags while you create content on the board. Pinterest uses hashtags just like Instagram, which can be a great way to increase the presence of your content in their searches of interest.

    For example, if you have a dropshipping store related to selling rollerblades, you can use hashtags such as #skateforlife, #rollerblades, #customerollerblades, etc.

7. Collaborate With Other Pinterest Influencers

Influencers found on social media platforms are some of the most popular web celebrities that can help you boost your sales and marketing campaigns. Furthermore, they are quite popular among online users. Any item that popular influencers tell their followers to buy sells like hotcakes.

A benefit of collaborating with influencers is that they are accessible to both big and small businesses. Several brands have been able to produce huge traffic through Pinterest influencers alone. You can collaborate with such bloggers and influencers and take the benefit of increasing your followers through their reach.

When users see and hear their favorite celebrity or people sharing their positive views about a company or product, they often end up purchasing a product. That's one of the many ways of using social media to improve dropshipping business. You can use it to your advantage in various ways.

To collaborate with such influencers, you will have to search for them. Some new ones may review your products for free, while others may ask for a price to promote your niche product. Another option that some influencers can provide to promote your products is if they get to keep your products.

You can also sell products on Pinterest by making your pins display in the Pinterest Gifts option. This option is a drop-down menu listing items on Pinterest, which show products in price-based groups. So, remember to add a price to the pins you own so that they can appear on the Gifts section, helping you earn more.

Is Pinterest Marketing for You?

DROPSHIPPING

Several ways exist on Pinterest that will let you sell your niche products. Increase your brand following using these ways so that your dropshipping business can flourish.

You can find tons of ways to increase your brand following via Pinterest, which will help you sell more. All you have to do is find creative ways to make new content to lure new customers.

Instagram Marketing

Instagram is a popular social media platform that can be used for marketing your dropshipping business effectively. Instagram has so many users that stay active on it every day. Naturally, that creates a huge marketplace filled with potential customers for you. And all you have to do is post videos and photos on that platform to engage with viewers. Even for a dropshipping business, Instagram can be worth exploring to promote your business.

Millions of viewers can see products posted by various businesses there. If you do post your products there, will that help you reach and sell to more people? Using Instagram as a marketing gateway can give your business impactful opportunities. All you need to do is research your business so that you can implement successful ways to promote your niche products.

In this section, let's discuss how Instagram marketing can be beneficial for your dropshipping business.

DROPSHIPPING

Why Use Instagram Marketing for Dropshipping?

There are several reasons to use Instagram marketing for your dropshipping business. Here are a few of them:

- **Large User Base**

Instagram has over 500 million active accounts, which are daily surfing on this incredible platform. If you have gone through their app, you will have noticed millions of posts shared every day. Imagine the number of likes, shares, and comments on all those posts daily.

Therefore, you can see how beneficial Instagram marketing is for dropshipping as a social media marketing platform with potential. Using Instagram can help you define the presence of your business at new levels. You can promote it several ways on this social media app, letting you reach more people efficiently.

- **Less Investment**

If you have an interesting niche to promote, you can publish posts related to the niche regularly on your Instagram page. Doing so will only cost you time and effort with a little bit of investment (mostly on internet connection). Instagram is famous for providing lots of organic traffic, which can be very beneficial for your business. It has so many active users who can convert into potential buyers at almost zero investment.

- **Competitive Advantage**

DROPSHIPPING

Most users who want to promote through social media channels rely on Facebook or Twitter to do so. A low percentage of those users choose Instagram to promote their products. That can be advantageous for you if you choose Instagram marketing because the competition is low there, though it might not stay like that for long. So, it's better if you prepare a marketing strategy to promote your dropshipping webstore through Instagram.

- **Visually Effective**

You can notice that Instagram is mostly a visual media sharing web and mobile app. Choosing images and videos over text-based content is much more appealing to viewers. Users are more interested in viewing such content as it is a convenient way to get information. Adding hashtags with these images further helps to get the images and videos to reach more people worldwide. So, if you post images and video content related to your niche products, you can gain potential followers and buyers.

- **Little Ad Costs**

Even though you can choose to promote your posts on Instagram through paid options, you don't need to spend money if you have interesting and unique posts to share with other users. As mentioned earlier, Instagram is one of the most effective platforms to generate organic traffic. And you can use this quality to improve your dropshipping business.

- **Simple to Use**

DROPSHIPPING

Unlike other social media platforms, Instagram doesn't require you to create complicated profiles. Setting up an account there is very easy, and you can instantly start posting media related to your products to promote your brand. You can open an individual account or business account without filling out too many details.

With the right approach, you can use Instagram to build a massive fan-following who can convert to potential buyers for you. That way, you can enjoy huge profits in the long term.

Now, let's see how you can create your own dropshipping business account on Instagram.

How to Create a Dropshipping Business Account on Instagram

Here are the steps:

1. Start by signing up with a new account on Instagram.

2. Choose a username relevant to your business. You can use your brand name, which will help users find you easily. It's also a good way to market your niche products.

3. Add a profile photo. Choose your brand logo, which is the most effective and relevant of all images.

4. Write a bio highlighting what your business is about. You will get 150 characters for it – so be

very concise and clear with the description. But writing a bio is optional. If you do not wish to disclose anything, you can do that too. Instead, you can just mention your website URL there. But we recommend adding a few words to let users know what your account is all about.

5. Connect your Instagram account to other sites like Facebook. This will be very advantageous to increase your reach on a variety of sites. Plus, you have the option to share created posts on all such sites, making it less time-consuming.

That's basically it – it's that simple. Now, let's discuss the hard part.

Why Is Your Instagram Strategy Not Very Effective?

Maybe you already have an Instagram page ready for your business, and you may be posting regularly to try to lure potential customers. But it might not work.

Let's look at some of the things you might be doing wrong when trying to market your dropshipping business with Instagram.

- **Lack of Unique Content**

Daily posts on Instagram will do your business no good if such posts are commonly found all over the social media platform. You want your customers to see rare and unique content that they have never seen before. Showing them images and videos uniquely related to your niche products will grab their attention, making them click on your posts and visit your webstore or site.

But it's easier said than done.

You have to invest your time in thinking of creative and effective ways to come up with posts. Moreover, the posts that you think of should be relevant to potential customers so they feel like engaging with your content.

- **Posting Content Irregularly**

Instagram requires you to be active on it so that people know of your existence. Your posts do not necessarily have to be daily, but you should follow a regular pattern when posting unique and effective content to share with users. Consistency is the key. Set a target of sharing a particular number of posts every week, which will help viewers connect with your Instagram page more often. Eventually, they will be curious enough to check out what products you have for them. It's a good rule to remember to be regular with your posts.

- **Not Being Public**

You have an Instagram account to share content with your viewers. But it would be useless if that account was not intended as a bridge to let viewers reach your online dropshipping store. This happens when you don't share relevant details related to your business account. You will have to disclose the details of your account so people can reach you and buy stuff. If you don't do that, you cannot expect your

DROPSHIPPING

business to monetize **even** a bit. Keep the account public, and let the business roll in with time.

- **Neglecting Instagram Tools and Filters**

The various filters and tools present on Instagram are there to help create more engaging content to share with users. Many might think of it as extra work, but it is worth the effort to do it. Using quality filters can help you make your images and videos stand out from the crowd. After all, this social media platform's primary content material is in the form of images. Always aim to use high-quality images with various tools and filters to enhance their appeal.

- **Avoid Interacting with Users**

Your level of interaction on Instagram can decide how well you perform on this portal. If you avoid answering comments and queries posted by users on your content, you will lose their interest. They might get irritated due to your lack of interaction, which will make them leave your page eventually. You need to treat your customers well. Several of them may turn out to be long-term customers for you.

- **Neglecting Hashtags**

Instagram also uses the power of hashtags to generate large viewership on daily posts. Using them is one of the primary ways of ensuring a wider reach. If you neglect using hashtags completely, your posts may not be visible to the people who show interest in your niche. Even if your content is engaging, your posts may never reach potential viewers if you do not use any hashtags, as hashtags will certainly catch the attention of such users.

Now, let's end this section on Instagram marketing for helpful dropshipping tips.

Tips to Optimize an Instagram Dropshipping Account

You can use several types of strategies to improve your performance on Instagram, which will help your business flourish.

Some of the popular tips are explained for you below:

- **Use Appropriate Hashtags**

We mentioned earlier that hashtags are important when you post on Instagram. But you cannot just pepper your posts with hashtags. You should focus on choosing relevant and trendy ones that can help give your post a boost. Note that trendy hashtags do not have to be super popular, as the content keeps updating in those community pages fast, and the chances are that your posts get squashed in between the old and new posts.

Instead, choose a hashtag with a decent following, so your posts are visible to users for a couple of hours. That way, people interested in the hashtag will find your post and start liking and following it. So, optimize the posts with relevant hashtags after planning their search volume. If you like, you can also use hashtags that your rivals use.

Plus, they should be relevant to your brand so it can increase its reputation among your potential audience. Another thing

DROPSHIPPING

you can do is create your own brand hashtag. Use it in every post that you share on your Instagram page. With time, people will start following and using it in their posts to make your brand more popular, eventually boosting your business reach.

- **Utilize the Instagram Tools**

You can use plenty of tools on Instagram that can help optimize your marketing strategies. Some of them are texting, calling, and emailing. To do that, switch to your business account, which gives you access to promotional activities and insights.

With insights, you get to know everyone who follows your page and which posts are showing the best results. You can also use apps like Followers+ to keep track of all the details. It will show you who follows and unfollows you, how many likes you have in total, and more. Analyzing the insights can be very effective in helping you understand which posts are engaging. That way, you can create more posts like those to attract viewers.

Promote tool will let you promote the posts that are popular among users. Such posts show good engagement when you pay a little to increase their reach on Instagram. Through this tool, you also get to choose your targeted audience, which will help generate more traffic to your webstore.

- **Focus on Visuals**

As stated above, focus on improving the images and videos you share on your Instagram page. You want them to be high-

DROPSHIPPING

quality and appealing, so users instantly feel attracted to them. To achieve that, you can use filters, editing tools, color corrections, borders, and more. The idea is to make your work noticeable. Be creative while maintaining quality in your work.

- **Interact With the Users**

Your posts will start seeing comments and likes. If the comments are positive, acknowledge them. If they are negative, ask them how you can improve. If they have questions, answer them with positivity. What's important is that you interact with them and let them remember you and your Instagram page. Your activity should never be limited to just uploading your posts. Engagement is important so that your audience becomes fans of your work. That can help you gain their trust, giving them more reason to buy products from you.

- **Use Brand Name as Your Username**

You would want your brand name to become popular among your audience. To do that, make sure you choose your brand name as your Instagram account's profile name. That's the first way users are going to recognize you and your business.

You might have a long name for your dropshipping business, and adding a full name might not be interesting for your username. Try to shorten it in a catchy way but still make it related to your brand name. The popularity of your brand and its reputation is all in your hands.

- **Post Smart**

DROPSHIPPING

You will have to decide the right time to share your posts with the target audience when they are free to surf on the social media platform. The idea is to make sure your posts are as engaged as possible. To ensure that, you will have to avoid posting when users are busy with jobs, chores, and personal work. If they miss your post updating at the right time, your marketing posts will all be in vain.

Posting content at the right time when the users are active on Instagram may prove beneficial for your business. Furthermore, when you post strategically, keeping in mind the activity of your followers and users, you can get more engagement on your content. And, if your post becomes popular, it can get featured on the Instagram Explore feed as well.

Additional Ways to Market Your Dropshipping Business

Becoming a successful dropshipping entrepreneur will require you to add more effort to marketing in multiple ways. We discussed a few significant ones in the previous sections – now, we will look into some additional ways to promote your dropshipping business.

Besides, marketing is the main operation required by you as a dropshipper because the third-party supplier mostly handles the shipping and inventory.

Diversify your marketing strategy so that you can reach a larger audience in various demographic locations, communities, groups, and more. Promotion is all about catching the viewer's eye, so they get to know what you have to offer them.

DROPSHIPPING

Let's look at some of these ways:

- **Go for Paid Promotion**

This is one of the most convenient ways of marketing a business online. Paid promotion is often a great way to start a new business. With this strategy, you invest the money to let the marketing platform promote your posts to people you want to target.

Paid advertising will give you the spotlight from the start, no matter what your firm's reputation is at its current stage. You have several online places to promote your dropshipping business. Some of these include social media platforms like Facebook, Instagram, Twitter, and more. Besides these, the most popular one is Google, which gives your post the top spot in its search results for keywords related to your business.

- **Promote Via YouTube**

Customers who want to buy products from your dropshipping store will want to know more about the product's quality before they purchase it. The best way to display your products' quality, performance, and other attributes is by sharing videos about them through YouTube.

Over 85% of consumers want to buy products after seeing reviews about them on YouTube. Creating a YouTube channel dedicated to showing your niche products' practical usage is a great idea. The videos should give viewers detailed information about the products you have, to feel more motivated to buy products from you.

DROPSHIPPING

You can also create videos related to how to use the products, maintenance videos, tips to improve their efficiency, and more. It's all about creating unique content that viewers will be interested to learn about.

Another way to promote through YouTube is by paying an influencer who has many subscribers and viewers on the platform. Let them review your products with positive feedback. YouTubers greatly influence their followers, which can trigger record-breaking sales of products at a moment's notice.

Using YouTube for marketing is an effective strategy that will undeniably make your dropshipping business flourish in the long term.

- **Join Online Communities**

This is also an effective way to promote your business and products, and it involves a simple strategy to promote in an online community filled with your target audience. Such communities could be present on various social media platforms, like Facebook groups, Telegram, Slack, Reddit, online forums, or even local groups participating in regular meetings.

One can even join websites like Quora, focusing on answering queries that people may have about products, services, or any other thought. But you cannot market your business straightaway like a spammer. Instead, become an active member, interacting and engaging with the community's online members to increase your reputation first.

DROPSHIPPING

Platforms like Reddit do not even let people post anything unless they increase their Karma points and then promote something. Plus, the promotion strategy on such communities should not look like a sales pitch. You should focus on empathizing with the members rather than irritating them with your presence in their group.

- **Use Email Marketing**

This strategy works quite well when you have a decent following or a list of subscribers signing up for email newsletters and notifications from you. As a business promoter, you don't want to lose touch with your target audience and should email them from time to time, telling them about your latest offers, which is an effective strategy.

You should strategize email marketing in such a way that it is frequent but not too frequent. Otherwise, your audience may feel irritated and feel like you are a spammer. Your emails should not be like sales pitches to inform your viewers about buying stuff from you. Focus on creating engaging content that provides valuable information to the reader.

Add content that teaches them about things related to the products. Create tips, guides, and benefits posts in the form of newsletters that have a compelling call-to-action, taking your viewers to your dropshipping store, so it is interesting to read. You can also give them discounts through these emails so that your subscribers can come to visit your store to get more products.

- **Focus on SEO**

DROPSHIPPING

Besides paid promotions, you can work on optimizing your dropshipping webstore, social media pages, and other accounts featuring your business. SEO is all about displaying appealing content that users would love to read. Bear in mind that search engine optimizing may not give you instant results. It can take some time before your content gains authority over your target niche.

To work on your website and social media pages' SEO, use various marketing tools that can help you target your crowd effectively. Many of the tools, both online and offline, have free versions available. Some of them are Google Keyword Planner, SEMrush, Moz, YOAST, UberSuggest, and Google Trends. You can always invest in professional accounts later when you get used to the dashboard and features, which will help make the content stand out from the crowd.

If you do not have time to focus on the search engine optimization of your dropshipping store on your own, invest in an SEO agency that can help you gain popularity. Professional SEO optimizers can help you increase your search engine rankings many times if done correctly. Hiring or outsourcing a brilliant SEO team to handle the marketing can make your work a lot easier but at a cost. If you can spend money on hiring pros, do use it.

- **Word of Mouth**

It's certainly one of the most conventional marketing strategies, and it can do wonders if you execute it correctly. By simply telling people about your business during get-togethers, meetings, and other social gatherings, you can gain many

DROPSHIPPING

potential customers for your dropshipping store. They will also be impressed by recommendations from your customers.

Don't start marketing your store instantly, which may seem inappropriate. Instead, make a habit of introducing your dropshipping business after talking about the person you want to target. Smartly mention your business as if it came out spontaneously. That way, it feels like it has naturally become part of the conversation.

If you can satisfy your customers with your dropshipping products, they will talk and mention them to their friends, family members, and other individuals they know. As a result, the marketing strategy can create a chain reaction, giving your webstore an incredible boost free of cost.

- **Get Reviews on Your Products**

When customers buy products from your portal, make sure to acknowledge and thank them for the purchase. Also, encourage them to give testimonials and reviews on the purchased products, so you know if your product is helpful or whether it needs any improvement.

Some eCommerce sellers invest in influencers to get reviews on their products, as mentioned before. You can apply that strategy as well. While people have been known to get paid reviews, try to avoid that. If you are selling high-quality products, you will barely need to do a paid promotion of any kind.

DROPSHIPPING

A Tip: Remember that marketing is a game with many chances and opportunities. Using the ones that will add more value to your business will make it worth your time. Find the right marketing strategies based on your niche and targeted audience.

Find the people who can help you spread the word for free or at a budgeted cost. Furthermore, invest in platforms that can give your store a wider audience. Combining strategies can have a great impact on your business for sure.

Remember that dropshipping businesses can work best when you use all the opportunities available to you because the market is competitive. There will be thousands of competitors ready to snatch your customers and vice-versa. Try finding customers and market your products to them using good ethics. Applying such a strategy will ensure they stay with you for the long term.

CHAPTER 6

SCALING YOUR BUSINESS

This chapter will talk about an important parameter that will superficially work for taking your dropshipping business to the next level. Here, you will learn about the scaling process and ways to achieve it for business growth and expansion. It will only help your business when you are selling like crazy. You never know what is going to happen in the coming days.

Problems may hamper your business' sales, and that is where earlier planning of business scaling will work.

But!

Before we discuss ways to scale your dropshipping business, you need to understand the concept well. Some entrepreneurs even mistake 'Scaling' with the word 'Growth,' which has a strikingly different meaning. However, we will discuss it in the latter part.

So!

What do you understand by the term "Scaling/Scalability?'

DROPSHIPPING

Scaling or Scalability is derived from the Latin word "Scale," which means "to climb by." In the business sense, scaling means taking a bigger leap toward revenue generation or growing your business.

In general, when a company scales, it soars high in terms of revenue so that its losses make little impact. This way, the company does not only grow but will scale as well.

However, scaling a business is directly proportional to the capacity your business can endure. Therefore, before you actually plan to leap higher, you need a basic understanding of your resources, delivery capacity, infrastructure, and much more.

Once you have a thorough understanding of your capacity, you will need to create success milestones. Remember, if you fail to analyze your resources (delivery capacity, infrastructure, human resource, and other parameters), you may have a long list of failed deliveries, miscommunications, and worst of all, "unhappy customers."

But don't worry! We will teach you strategically about achieving scale without any loopholes. Before that, let me explain "how scaling is different from growth?"

How is Scaling Different From Growth?

We have often seen folks use the terms "scaling" and "growth" interchangeably. However, the two business terms have a distinct difference that every entrepreneur must understand. Learning the crucial difference will help in the strategic planning of business scaling.

DROPSHIPPING

Next time if some businessman uses "Growth" to represent the "Scalability" of his business in front of you, correct him right away.

Also, explain to him the definition that says when a company grows, it earns revenue by investing new funds in discrete sectors like promotions, human resource hiring, etc. In this case, the company's gains and losses are evened out without adding more values into gains.

On the contrary, scalability defines the state of revenue generation where a company outpaces the liabilities and losses, adding more figures into its gains.

Having said that, while you plan your dropshipping startup and make strategies for its revenue generation, you must devise strategies to achieve scaling rather than growth. This way, you will not only increase the efficiency of your business but will keep the revenue safe when the market conditions are less favorable.

Steps for Scaling Your Dropshipping Business

It is worth considering scaling your dropshipping business. It will create a sustainable environment for long-term benefits unaffected by the ups and downs of the market.

However, you might be a little skeptical about how the scaling model will work. You may continuously ask the same questions poverty and over in your mind as to whether it will produce favorable results or not.

DROPSHIPPING

Well, I would suggest you stay neutral and optimistic about the scaling process. If you plan your branding, lower product acquisition costs, and take the help of online advertising techniques, you will be successful in creating the sustainable environment you yearned for.

Therefore, stop being skeptical about it and move with the process of scaling. You will require a few important steps to achieve this target.

1. **Identify Your Business Milestones**

When you identify your business milestones, you practically expect that you have limited funds to invest (it is similar with every startup these days). Therefore, you need to invest well and hit the timeline before you run out of cash.

Here, it would not be wrong to say that you need to work out a roadmap to define milestones to hit within a given timeline. And even if your cash gets low, you can plan to fundraise and buy some extra time to achieve your milestones.

Further, it would be advisable not to think of valuation as a number that only increases. You can do a valuation by measuring your reduced risks and ease of doing business over time.

2. **Focus More on Risk Reducers**

Reduced risks mean healthy growth. If your business has fewer risks, you will be more focused on other attributes to increase growth rather than planning out to curb risks with passing the time. But do you have any idea about the risk reducers? Well,

DROPSHIPPING

it is an attribute that can help your business reduce risks for investors and customers. You can take their help and plan out references for your potential investors and customers. The risk reducer will have data-backed proof for your potential investors so that they have faith in your brand for future investment, whereas, for customers, they will have data-backed proof of the benefits associated with your products backed up by previous sales.

3. Focus on Increasing the Sales

Your business solely flourishes on the daily sales your organization achieves. The more orders you get, the more sales are added to your lists. But! Where will you get the bookings from?

Well, there is nothing very explicit to do. You can achieve a good number of orders by expanding your business reach, planning new marketing strategies, and promoting your brand.

Your ideal milestone should be equating the number of orders to the Average Rate of Return (ARR).

4. Identify Your Target Audience and Loyal Customers

Your business is nothing without your loyal customers. However, this process takes time. Therefore, you should first start gaining customers who will slowly become loyal to your valuable services.

Customer growth starts by channelizing your products to the target market. A few steps that will help midway are –

DROPSHIPPING

- Selection of target customer base
- Start with product promotions
- Communicate your product's worth

All these three steps will help you fuel the product sales and gains. You can also deploy a feedback system to get considerable input from your users to study your buyers' behavior. Once you get the feedback, it will be easy to solve your sales issues and drawbacks.

5. Optimize Your Products According to the Ideal Buyers

Increasing sales by getting more consumers is an ideal process with time-to-time ignition. You can do this systematically by optimizing the pages where your product is promoted. If your customers have more inclination toward social media, run daily broadcasts and ask for social media reviews. You can also run blogs and publish articles about your products from time to time if you wish to have more of a presence among educated customers.

6. Keep the Number of Hired Salespeople in Check

It is good to have a robust human resource to back the company's process, but most entrepreneurs hire too quickly without thinking much about the aftereffect in the long run. Sometimes, hiring staff without any need can backfire and use up the company's funding.

DROPSHIPPING

Initially, you should hire staff that can help you with all processes. You can also call them "pathfinder and trailblazers." They will act as a salesperson or an administrator when required. Their multi-functionality will reduce the cost of staffing and add to more gains.

Actionable Tips to Have a Positive Scaling Process

Many factors affect a dropshipping business in a certain way when implemented. In this part, you will learn about such factors and impacts on dropshipping business scaling.

- **Strengthen Your Brand Reputation**

Before you take over the market, you need to establish your business as a popular brand. This is an unspoken rule which your dropshipping business will have to follow.

Well, you can indeed generate a lot of revenue by investing through a strategic investment sales plan. However, initially, your strong branding will matter to differentiate your business from less established sellers.

When a brand is well-planned and steady in its success, it can achieve more using fewer resources. For example, if you already have an established branding among potential buyers, you will not need to invest in high-paying ads and promotions. Your ad costs will be lower, simultaneously lowering the product acquisition cost.

As you know, a dropshipping business heavily depends on the sellers you procure products from. Any hiccups in the market could shatter the earned branding. Therefore, you will need to

DROPSHIPPING

remain consistent about the changes in the market and develop new product lines along with the old ones.

Note: Your popularity among buyers is the critical factor to aid in strong branding. As strong as your products and services are, payout reputation depends on your branding. But you also remember that every time a product line fails, your investment in advertising and chances of strong branding will go back to square one. Strong branding will always remain the first parameter for scaling!

- **Have Good Control Over Supply Chains**

Supply chains can make or break the backbone of any dropshipping business, which may adversely impact the scaling process.

As you are very well informed that the whole dropshipping business model depends on procuring items on-demand from producers and delivering them to consumers, the slightest mismanagement in supply chains will kill the delivery speed and affect the appeal of your business negatively.

As you fail to deliver the items on-time to your potential consumers, they will move away, which will affect your revenue and scaling process.

Therefore, before you work on bringing in more and more orders for your product lines, have firm control over your supply chains. Also, make sure the producers or suppliers you choose to work with have a wide range of items going with your brand, scalable inventories, and quality products.

DROPSHIPPING

Note: You will need to get in touch with all reputed suppliers to establish a successful dropshipping business in a particular industry. You will have to keep following the latest trends to see noticeable changes.

Also, changing your product suppliers will often limit the goodwill of your dropshipping business. You will have to remain consistent with the quality you have been delivering so far. It will drop the revenue margin very strikingly, affecting the overall scalability process if you cannot maintain your good reputation.

- **Achieve Customer Satisfaction**

A satisfied customer is the key to a strong business. This rule applies to the dropshipping business model as well. If you focus on satisfying your buyers' product requirements, your dropshipping business will become trustworthy to your targeted niche. And if you even once dare to overlook the importance à of listening to an unhappy customer, his negative experience could snowball the respect and goodwill you have earned so far.

Managing consumer grievances should be engraved as a core value so that it will not affect the brand's value in the long run. The smallest spark online could damage the popularity and loyal customers you have earned so far, along with monetary revenues.

You can realize the impact by considering the example as explained here.

DROPSHIPPING

Suppose that you require a total of 2 weeks to procure a product and deliver it successfully to the consumer's doorstep. Now, let's assume that you made a total of 900 sales within the first two weeks and earned $50 per product sale. The earning per product has to be deducted for liabilities associated like $15 for advertising and promotions and $10 for initial product purchase. After excluding all the liabilities, you are left with $25 as your profit (a happy time to celebrate, of course).

However, this happiness may not last long if your consumers did not like the product and want to return it. Your earned profit will roll over to zero, incurring you a heavy loss. You should note that you still have not calculated the cost of shipping, payment transaction fees, bad relations with your supplier, etc.

Initially, this loss would be the most significant setback for the business scaling process and could bring your enthusiasm and revenue down significantly.

Therefore, you should understand the value of customer satisfaction and take strategic measures to achieve it. The best you can do to pipeline 100% customer satisfaction is to run high-level and 24/7 customer support. The customers should be able to reach you at any point in time. This will avoid the issues of product returns and bad publicity.

Note: The customer support panel must be well-versed with customer handling etiquette so that unhappy customers are returned happily with a satisfactory experience.

DROPSHIPPING

- **Plan to Re-Engage Consumers With Retargeting Ads**

Every seller, especially one from a dropshipping business, loves customers who come back for more. It is pure bliss that all your product lines are popular among customers, and they prefer to order from you.

But! How easy do you find it to achieve?

It depends on the seller. If you provide outstanding and quality products, your customer base will be more tempted to try every option available to them through you.

Again, the question arises – how will you reengage the old customer base to try new products? The answer is "with the help of retargeting ads and re-engagement." All you need is to get a strategic plan carved out for re-engagement and carried out under expert guidance.

You can take help from Facebook Ads, Google Ads, and social media broadcasting to produce more sales while maintaining the cost per campaign. Once you have successfully invested in re-engagement plans, you can, later on, invest in retargeting ads and increase the chances of brand visibility.

Every time your customer base hears of your new product lines, they will be motivated enough to at least land on your website to learn about them. Rest assured, if your new product lines have that necessary charm to tempt them, they will immediately place further orders with you.

- **Develop Business Along With New Product Lines**

DROPSHIPPING

It is good to have diverse product lines so that every customer returns satisfied from your doorstep. However, you cannot invest all your time and money in developing new product ideas. Besides, you will also need to develop your business and strengthen its base.

As a dropshipping business owner, you will have to work out all business elements and take them all together as a whole. Otherwise, the dream of a scalable business will go no further, requiring more investment and time.

Therefore, it would be highly beneficial to sit back and analyze your long-term business strategies and optimization opportunities. As you focus on business development, you will make new discoveries to expand and optimize your dropshipping business.

Note: Once you have a full-blown customer base and an ever-expanding sales graph, you may not have the time to improve or optimize any parameter associated with your business.

- **Achieve Low-Cost Customer Acquisition**

Cost of customer acquisition or customer acquisition costs (CAC), as you may like to think of it, defines the investment made by you to attract customers and convert them into buyers. It is evident that the low cost of customer acquisition will result in higher revenue, and fortunately, there is no shortage of such opportunities.

If you go out onto the market and research low-cost ways to acquire customers, you will be surprised by the multitudes of options available like influencer marketing, affiliate marketing, content marketing, etc.

But the success will depend upon your products' reach and how efficiently it is marketed.

Note: CAC (customer acquisition costs) are variable and keep changing over time. There may be some methods that superficially worked earlier but did not even spark interest now. Therefore, testing will be required every time you plan to work out a new campaign.

- **Make Content Marketing Your Ally**

Content marketing is a low-cost and authoritarian practice of customer acquisition and branding. The best part about this practice is that it works for every business sector and elevates brands.

Therefore, spare yourself some time for content marketing and make it your best ally for branding and customer acquisition. Fortunately, you will not have to create a different platform to make it work. It will utilize your website and social media handles to publish authoritative content and attract customers.

The whole process could be made easy by an eCommerce SEO expert. He will plan strategies and direct them so that you will receive organic traffic and achieve lead conversion. A well-informed SEO expert will bring all aspects of content marketing and promotion together to work coherently for your dropshipping business goals. He may utilize the power of

DROPSHIPPING

content on landing pages, blogs, and reviews to bring customers to your website.

The rest of the work will be done by your diverse product lines and their quality!

Note: Content marketing is a good strategy for customer acquisition, but it will not show results overnight. If you start investing your money in content marketing now, you will harness its benefits in the future.

- **Utilize Web Analytics to Understand Your Audience**

You cannot randomly sell your product to anybody. As a dropshipping business owner, you will have to collect data, analyze it and make data-driven plans to acquire customers and match their tastes.

However, the path is not that straightforward. You will need the help of web analytics to get familiar with your potential and ideal audiences to grow as a more popular and reliable business. With the help of data, you will understand your target audience and drive their attention toward your products using Keyword Research and Google trends.

There are many campaigns available like Facebook Analytics and Google Analytics to realize such goals. However, you will need a helping hand to predict the trends and help you sway customers.

- **Automate the Process of Order Fulfillment**

DROPSHIPPING

Technology has rapidly changed the course of online selling over time. Receiving orders manually has lost weight, and automation has taken over. Precisely, this the time when you either do it or lag behind with backlogs of orders and pending dreams of scaling your business.

Manual order fulfilling and scaling of business will not go hand in hand because manual processes are always on the riskier side, leading to errors and time consumption.

By automating the whole process of receiving the order and delivering it without being personally involved, you will save quality time spared for other tasks that remain unattended to most of the time.

Moreover, it will be a significant step toward scaling your dropshipping business. It will reduce human errors, aid smooth order fulfillment, and help you achieve speedy delivery.

- **Automate the Process of Order Tracking**

From receiving orders to dispatching them and until the orders have successfully reached the customer, there are many instructions to be given and communication involved.

A person needs to be alert of any query placed regarding delivery and delivery timing, simultaneously looping delivery agents and managing the logistics. The whole process eats quality time which could be shifted to handling matters of much value.

DROPSHIPPING

For instance, you can make a portal where customers can log in their details and track their shipment online. This will reduce the need for your involvement, especially when dealing with transit-related queries.

Automatic emails, an online tracking platform or SMSs, will all create a huge impact on the automation process and aid scaling of your business.

- **Establish Good Relations With Supplier**

A good relationship with your suppliers is a key aspect of a dropshipping business. You cannot succeed in the business without a fool-proof backing of suppliers offering low prices and bulk products.

Therefore, you should nurture a loyal and healthy relationship between all your big and small suppliers so that you can grow and expand with them.

A healthy relationship will pave the chances of better understanding and price negotiations when needed.

Note: Always keep in touch with your existing suppliers and maintain healthy communication. You can also prepare a monthly report of profits generated for them so that they will keep you as a priority when compared to other dropshipping sellers.

- **Keep Experimenting with New Strategies**

Scaling a dropshipping business requires fortune and effort in the same ratio. You cannot just invest the money and wait for

DROPSHIPPING

things to work out. You will have to keep researching new strategies, and you a keep yourself informed of potential business expansion.

Also, don't be disheartened when a strategy does not work for you. There is no written rule that if a plan worked for one company, it would work for you as well. This is an era of experimenting, and hence, you should keep exploring new ideas and try converting them into a successful dropshipping business.

Note: You will need a creative vision to formulate new ideas. You can even consult with your suppliers about their new product lines, which you can sell through your dropshipping business.

Challenges That You Might Face While Scaling Your Dropshipping Business

Dropshipping has been a popular and successful business model with proven case studies. However, many entrepreneurs do state about the hardships they faced while scaling their businesses.

The reason each entrepreneur stated was different but essential to learning and never repeating the same errors while scaling the business.

In this section of the book, all those setbacks/limitations faced while scaling a dropshipping business are collectively explained with possible solutions.

- **Time Crisis – No Time for Self and Business**

DROPSHIPPING

I still remember talking to a close friend and a dropshipping owner about his professional and personal life. According to him, "he could not find enough time for himself and other important tasks related to business administration because he used to be busy managing customer queries, service calls, and replying to emails all day long." He was soon sleep-deprived and too exhausted to even think of any new product ideas or plans.

I would suggest not being like him and acting smart when you see your orders rising to 60 and more. You can be a multitasker. However, you should not try this because a scaling business will require more of your time to invest in far important directions.

What Should You Do Instead?

Hire a few talented people and build a team of virtual assistants. You can even hire a manager to coordinate with virtual assistants and help in the smooth workflow. Once you are done with the selection, train your new recruits according to the schedule you followed and step back to see their performance for a short time.

Over time with expert guidance, your team will learn to excel in the jobs they were hired to do. Your team members must have an understanding of tasks depending upon your dropshipping business niche.

They should at least be good at:

1. Handling Grievances

2. Spreadsheet editing

3. Copywriting

4. Content editing

5. Customer handling

6. Logistics

7. Listings

- **Suppliers Are Not Able to Scale With You**

As you plan to scale and process a larger volume of daily orders, your suppliers may not be scaled enough to help you achieve your aims.

Therefore, before you plan to scale your business and process a larger volume of orders daily, you will need to escalate the number of suppliers delivering the same products with the same quality. If you fail to do this, your business may hit rock bottom and bring you disappointment from customers and incurring losses.

What Should You Do Instead?

Understand every supplier's capabilities and ask them about required changes. If possible, help them automate the process of order fulfillment and be capable of handling larger volumes of orders.

DROPSHIPPING

If you have suppliers that aren't capable of effectively matching your scaling abilities, keep them in reserve and hire more suppliers. However, you should make sure that the quality delivered is managed well.

Don't ever freeze or create a dispute with any supplier!!

- **Suppliers** Incapable of Coping With Automation

Not every supplier out there is "Jack of all Trades." Many suppliers out their lack a basic understanding of technology. Forget about them being able to handle automatic order fulfillment and tracking processes. Actually, such suppliers could be a big limitation in your business scaling process.

What Should You Do Instead?

Make your suppliers aware of automated order fulfillment and tracking. Take some time and help them understand the whole process and the associated benefits. You can also inform them about the Five-Star Ratings given by customers when they efficiently follow the entire process.

In the long run, managing automation will make customers less anxious about your services and develop trust. This achievement will help you gain those 6 figure rewards which you have planning to achieve every day. Solving this major setback will be a significant milestone in the process of scaling your dropshipping business.

- **Trusting New Suppliers More Required**

DROPSHIPPING

Often it is difficult for business (you may or may not fall into this category) owners to judge a worthy supplier among unworthy ones. They generally tend to trust a new supplier with big orders and get disappointed when they fail to meet goals.

In that case, the failure harms the dropshipping business's credibility as well as losing existing clientele.

What Should You Do Instead?

When you add a new supplier to your business list, make sure you start with fewer bookings in the beginning. Later, when you have spent more than six months establishing a fail-proof and cordial relationship with your new supplier, you can increase the bookings and let the process run smoothly.

Being a dropshipping business owner, you will have to be careful and skeptical for good reasons. Until you have spent more than six months working with the same supplier, you will never know their actual capabilities and skills at handling bookings efficiently.

- **Lacking Patience and Persistence**

A Dropshipping business requires persistence and patience. In fact, not only this business model but all require persistence and patience. It will take time, investment, and a lot of effort to convert this business into a profitable one. And if you think that you are not that patient, leave the idea and move on to a different profession. You can try your hand with forex trading. (Pun intended!)

DROPSHIPPING

What Should You Do Instead?

Chalk out a basic plan and set small milestones to achieve. Unless you have spent all those calculated years building and nurturing the business, don't complain. If your strategies are well-designed and fool-proof, your business will work, and you will start to earn six figures daily.

- **High Prices of Dropshipping Products**

Why would anyone ever buy a product from your dropshipping store when it is available at a much lower price on other stores?

If you counter-back the question with the UBER quality you may provide, there is no match between cheap pricing and quality. All customers (except a few) prefer buying the same product from other stores, providing comparatively cheaper rates. However, if you have a great reputation, they won't mind spending more.

What Should You Do Instead?

Selling high-priced products is not a bad thing at all. However, it could be when you have more competitors preying on your potential customers. You will need to keep looking for information about your competitors' product lines, offer good prices, and make variations accordingly.

Once you have a strategic plan ready concerning your competitors' expected moves, you will be able to pitch efficiently, offering better deals. and budget sales.

DROPSHIPPING

Meanwhile, keep the high-priced products in continuation but only for high-ticket clients. This way, you will get large orders and earn an adequate profit.

- **Make Customers Wait for Days to Receive Their Orders**

It was once a huge deal to receive orders after a wait of 2 to 3 days or even a week. Nowadays, every eCommerce business has evolved by reforming and reducing delivery times. Amazon put the final nail in the coffin by offering Prime Deliveries.

Therefore, dropshippers, including you, will also have to evolve and match up with the flow. You will have to research ways to reduce the delivery time and build your service credibility.

If you can reduce the delivery time, your scaling goals will be far from being achieved.

What Should You Do Instead?

If you have significant suppliers from China, you cannot do anything but propose a delivery deadline within 20-25 days. It may exceed that or decrease in different situations. However, there are still many ways to work out quick delivery, like switching standard deliveries for ePacket.

As you order through ePacket, you get an exact estimation of delivery dates which can be further given to customers rather than bluffing them with random numbers.

DROPSHIPPING

DROPSHIPPING

CHAPTER 7

HOW TO EARN MORE SOURCES OF INCOME

The Dropshipping business model is no doubt a game-changer for generating passive income. As the business grows, you can quit your 9 to 5 job to become a full-time entrepreneur.

But dropshipping is not the only model that can help you earn a handsome fortune. There are many other business models and ideas which will work as well as dropshipping. In this chapter, you will learn about such business models and prerequisite tips to use them effectively.

Affiliate Marketing

Have you ever referred a product or service to your friends, neighbor, or even distant relatives? Do you have any idea that you could have earned perks if you had channelized those referrals?

DROPSHIPPING

Affiliate marketing is all about that – earning handsome perks by referring new clients to needy businesses, service providers, etc.

This practice has shaped into a fully-fledged business model where people refer and earn 4-5 digit numbers every day. The digits may exceed that in the case of a popular affiliate marketer with many followers.

You can sum up affiliate marketing as a process of earning commissions while referring to or marketing a company's products and services on a profitable level. The sales made under affiliate marketing are tracked via affiliate links as used by customers to buy products.

How Does the Affiliate Marketing Model Work?

Affiliate marketing utilizes unique links which help sellers track the affiliates responsible for particular sales. In the whole model, there are three important aspects around which the process revolves. The three aspects are -

1. **Seller and Product Creators**

The seller in affiliate marketing is an essential entity because he is the base of the pyramid. A seller could be any service provider, vendor, product creator, manufacturer, or retailer with a small or a large enterprise. He can have versatile product niches, including household items, furniture, clothes, beauty products, electronics, or even any service industry like a salon, beauty clinic, hospital, cosmetic surgeon, etc.

DROPSHIPPING

The seller will be the one requiring affiliate promotion so that his products and services are promoted widely within a limited budget. As affiliate marketing is solely commission-based marketing, the seller would have to pay commission only on sold items.

In a more formal tone, you can call affiliate marketing a revenue-sharing model. Affiliate marketing will work great for dropshipping businesses as well.

2. The Affiliate or Advertiser

An affiliate marketer is a person who promotes the services and products of others on a revenue-sharing basis. An affiliate marketer could be a sole person or a company working in synch with sellers to promote their products and services.

Affiliates sway customers with creative ads and promotional gigs depending upon sellers' services and products. As he succeeds in getting services and products sold through his affiliate links, he gains the due revenue.

3. The Consumer

Without a good consumer base, the affiliate model will not survive in the long run. Customers are the key aspect needed to buy products and services via affiliate links. Generally, customers are not aware of them being a part of the affiliate model. They are oblivious about any such practices and purchase the product/service for their personal use.

DROPSHIPPING

However, a few affiliate marketers do share the affiliate marketing secret with their consumers and help them decide whether they genuinely wish to buy the product or not.

The Process

The whole process is relatively easy to understand but with some extra punch. A few people understand that the affiliate gets paid for the product buyer's purchase through an affiliate link.

However, the entire story is a little different. Affiliates get paid for the purchases made via their affiliate links, but there is a hidden angle. You can understand that angle by reading the example.

Let's say person A watches your daily promotions and reads your blogs. He reads about a pair of cool glasses one day and decides to buy them via your affiliate link. But, as soon as he visits the page, he feels like fulfilling the order after a little while. Meanwhile, he sees another product from the same website and adds both to the cart.

When he does checkout buying, two articles from the same website, the cookies show two purchases via the same link, and the affiliate earns for both sales even though only one was intended.

Critical Parameters to Succeed in Affiliate Marketing

Becoming an affiliate marketer seems like a cakewalk, but not in all aspects. Only a few people succeed with affiliate

DROPSHIPPING

marketing because they need to stand out from the crowd and promote the products and services a little creatively.

Not everyone with a website, social media presence, or blog with minimal followers can become an affiliate marketer. A true affiliate should understand the importance of a few key parameters, which are explained below.

- **Have a Good Knowledge About Sellers**

Not all affiliate programs pay well. Therefore, you need to know your sellers very well before joining their affiliate programs.

- **Develop a Trustworthy Rapport**

Promote products only if you wish to use them as well. This will create a trustworthy rapport among buyers. As you will intend to use the same product, they will be clear about the quality of the products and services.

- **Have a Good Understanding of Products and Services**

Many affiliate marketers tend to promote fluff about products and services to get them sold. Users can be fooled once, twice, or maybe three times. After the third time, you will lose them forever.

- **Create a Pool of Affiliate Products and Services**

You cannot spend your lifetime promoting a single product or service. This will do no good for your dream of earning a 6-

digit monthly income. Therefore, rather than sticking to only one product, create a pool and promote them altogether.

- **Keep Track of your Sales and Earnings**

When you have more than one affiliate running and making money for your growth and survival, make sure that you have a cross-check on every program's progress. It would be best if you kept up to date on popular programs working well with your crowd and resonating with their vibes.

Lesson to Learn

Like dropshipping businesses, affiliate marketing also involves time and effort to grow. You will have to burn the midnight oil to prosper a bond with your customers and brands.

<u>Drop Servicing</u>

When the dropshipping business model worked wonders, many entrepreneurs realized that they could easily clone the same model with other business prospects like the service industry, skill-based freelancing, etc.

They realized that "a business can get started without even paying set up costs, office space and hiring regular employees." As soon as the idea got widely accepted, many entrepreneurs came up with their startups related to different fields, including –

- IT consultancy and solutions
- Website building

DROPSHIPPING

- Digital Marketing
- Ad copywriting
- Video editing
- Video creation
- Animation
- Social media management
- Technical support
- Marketing
- SEO
- Facebook ads
- Copywriting
- Content writing
- Graphic Design

What is the Actual Concept Behind Drop Servicing?

Drop servicing is not a new concept but a successful concept of this era with many successful stories to tell. You can call it a blast from the past with a proven history. If we talk about defining the term for professional understanding, Drop Serving is a fancy term for "Outsourcing, Reselling and Service Arbitrage."

DROPSHIPPING

People operating through the drop servicing model don't fulfill the client's requirements by themselves. They outsource the work to freelancers or a company that has immense experience in the industry. Drop servicers play the role of middlemen in getting the job done. The client may or may not know about the service provider completing the task behind closed doors.

And if you are still not clear about the whole model, replace the word products with services in a dropshipping model. You will get a drop servicing business model.

How Drop Servicing Works

It's not too difficult to understand. There are three attributes to this model.

- **Customer (Needy of Services)**

The Customer is the entity that has the requirement of a certain task to be completed. It could be related to any service industry.

- **Drop Servicer (Connecting End)**

The drop servicer answers the query and ascertains how the customer can get the job done. He then looks for a service provider and gets the job completed.

- **The Service Provider (Completes the Job)**

The service provider is the entity that is doing the job behind the scenes. He only gets remuneration for the job devoid of the name. The service provider remains hidden in many aspects as the drop servicer does not reveal it.

In drop servicing, a drop servicer generally sells the services at higher prices while getting the tasks done at lower prices.

How to Get Started with Drop Servicing

- **Research Comes First**

The first and foremost thing involved in getting started with a drop service is research. You will need to research and make a list of priority services, which you will provide in the name of services. You can choose any service but need to make sure that you have quality service providers to fulfill the jobs.

- **Idealizing the Next Step**

Once you have done your research, you will have to choose one of the following ways to get started.

a) **Create a Drop Service Store or a Website**

There are two ways to create a store, 1) build a website, or 2) create a store on Shopify. Both will deal with the task of lead generation. If you decide to build a website, you will need the assistance of a good website designer.

If you choose to get started through a Shopify store, visit the Shopify portal and follow the instructions to create a store. As you create your store at Shopify, you get additional services like payment systems, marketing tools, SEO, email subscription, social media promotions, and ease of doing business.

b) Join Any Freelance Marketplace

If you don't choose Shopify and wish to enter a freelance marketplace, then the sky is the limit. These days, you can find many freelance marketplaces online, including Fiverr, Freelancer.com, People Per Hour, ProBlogger, UpWork, and Hubstaff Talent.

You can join these marketplaces and post jobs. Freelancers will bid to complete the project, and herby producing work for less than you charge your client, make money for you.

The biggest drawback of such platforms is that they charge a commission for the service they provide. The range varies from 10% to 20%. Fiverr charges 20% of the earnings of freelancers.

Are There Limitations in Drop Servicing?

Fortunately, there are no limitations for people who have expertise in more than one field. You will thrive exponentially if you have a lot of expertise in the chosen field. As you gain knowledge of the service you are planning to deal with, you will be able to sell the service within a good price range.

However, if you lack basic understanding and know nothing about the field, you won't survive long.

What Should Be the Roundabout Investment Required for Drop Servicing?

DROPSHIPPING

You will have to invest in two things, time and a good internet connection. Once you have these, you can even start for free. However, if you wish to start with a store, Shopify, or build your own website, it will cost time and money.

You will need an investment of $30 to start a Shopify store. However, you will need a minimum investment of $70 to get a static website developed for the drop service business.

Are There Courses Available to Learn Drop Servicing?

You may not find a reputed or official online course to learn how to run a drop service business. However, you can ask for help from experts in the dropshipping model as both work on the same premise. All you have to do is replace manufactured goods/products with services.

How Soon Can You Start Earning Money?

Earning money through a drop service business is a speedy process. It takes a week or less, depending upon the project completion date. As soon as you get the work done, payment is released.

But you will have to remain extra cautious about the quality of services being delivered. You will need to have highly experienced service providers working for you. Hiring newbies could have a significant toll on your overall rapport.

Blogging

The term blog is a shortened form of "Weblog," which is a combination of two words, "web" and "blog." Blogs were first introduced in the 1990s and were more popular for writing personal diaries on the internet.

People used to write blogs to provide readers with personal true-life stories and information. They used to write about their lives and moderate comments of readers. Gradually, it became a source to promote opinions in favor or against particular topics involving politics, food, music, current affairs, business, etc.

As soon as blogs became more popularized, blogging came into the limelight. Visionary entrepreneurs recognized it as a next-gen marketing advancement and included blogging as a new money-making model.

What Is Blog Marketing?

Blog marketing is the process of letting readers know about new arrivals, new features, and benefits of a particular product or series of products sold on the market. In the initial days, business owners had to manage blogs separately from their websites. However, a blog can be easily integrated with a website to work as a unit these days.

In blog marketing, the content makes the entire premise and pitch. Therefore, the content should be of outstanding quality Anne relevance to readers. Only if the content provided through blog marketing is original, influential, and SEO-optimized can it reach potential readers and thus fulfill its task.

DROPSHIPPING

Why Business Owners Prefer Blog Marketing?

Minimum funds are needed. You can start blog marketing with minimal investment, i.e., the cost of purchasing a domain and its hosting services. You can build your blog on WordPress or get customized services that may cost a little extra.

- **Simple to Use**

You don't have to be a very tech-savvy or 'know-it-all' kind of personality for blog marketing. If you have a basic knowledge of writing, editing, and handling CMS, you can start a professional-looking blog page.

- **Attract Organic Traffic**

If your blog's content is of great use to readers and is original, it will bring more traffic and authority. And a good author and higher page rank will increase the chances of potential customers finding you and purchasing through you.

- **Improves Search Engine Ranking**

Many business owners target blog marketing only to generate traffic and increase SERPs. They use blogs, especially for SEO and Google ranking.

- **Great for Gaining Trust and Business Credibility**

If you wish to become a blogger and do blog marketing, you need to come under the radar of business owners, product creators, and manufacturers. But the path is not as easy as it seems. You will have to work out your content and establish a

DROPSHIPPING

rapport as an expert in your chosen niche. As you succeed in making your worth felt to business owners, they will hire you for their product marketing through your blog.

Moreover, you can even start your blog to support your existing dropshipping business, if you run any. You can self-promote your product lines and increase your sales.

- **Creates Opportunities for Additional Revenue**

Well, you can also use blogging to generate extra revenue by offering space for advertising. This comes in the form of media like banners, videos, audio clips, or links.

How to Achieve Your Goals in Blog Marketing

Starting a blog and creating the whole setup for it can be managed within a few minutes. If you are adamant about starting it quickly, you need to get a domain, blog hosting services, and create a WordPress blog.

However, its ongoing management, content creation, and credibility building will be time-consuming. It could give results in six months or take a lot longer. But don't be overwhelmed because there are still a few factors that can speed up revenue generation through blog marketing.

The factors are defined below.

- **Create a Well-Researched Plan**

There will be many bloggers out there to give you strong competition. What can you do differently to beat them? If you haven't got a great answer to this question, you have a long way to go. Brainstorming will have an essential part to play here.

From the type of content (news, infographic, tips, how-to, etc.) to the duration of blog management (daily, weekly, or hourly), you will have to pre-plan everything and follow the same routine religiously.

- **Choose a Catchy Yet Meaningful Domain Name**

Readers will initially remember your blog for its catchy name. Therefore, you should choose a name that is easy to remember and search.

- **Prepare Several Blogs to Upload**

Initially, when you plan to go live online, make sure you have an inventory of blogs ready. It will be easier to grab people's attention, and they will need to read your blog for a certain time before building trust in you.

- **Market Your Blog on Various Sites**

Before you start blog marketing, you will need to market your blog to bring the desired traffic. You will have to start this process as soon as possible. You can market your blog on various websites with the help of backlinks and promote it on social media sites to increase the number of followers.

- **Indulge in the Comment Section**

DROPSHIPPING

As you see people taking an interest in reading your blog and commenting, make sure you are also active in replying. A one-on-one communication will help build your blog's credibility and gain the trust of readers.

- **Encourage Readers to Sign Up With Email**

One of your ultimate goals should be targeting more and more people and encouraging them to sign up. Once readers sign up, they are expressing their desire to be associated with you. You can use this opportunity later by motivating them to spend money through email broadcast of a new service or product arrival, new sale, or discount running on certain products.

Blog marketing has benefits and virtues to offer. You will realize this once you have started making money from your blog. Moreover, it can be beneficial in another way too. If you have a dropshipping or drop servicing business, you can associate it with your blog and promote it.

Optimize Your Plan to Scale the Right Way

Avoid using shortcuts and con moves to scale your dropshipping business. You need to create a system that comprises proper planning, the right systems, tools, and decent funding to make the most out of your business. Use the knowledge you have gained from this chapter and apply it smartly to give you a productive business.

Certainly, it can be hard to scale your dropshipping business. Remember that using strategies in the right way will make it easier to support the growth of your company considerably.

DROPSHIPPING

Know the Dropshipping Loopholes

No doubt, dropshipping feels like a simple business strategy that requires very few operations, making it convenient and quick. It may seem that the only thing a seller needs to do is get the product and promote it among the targeted audience. However, this business is not limited to just your experience, but your customer's experience as well. If you want to keep your dropshipping business afloat, you will have to be very careful with your input strategies.

Despite the benefits, there are so many loopholes that we should highlight. For instance, how will you know if your customer is delighted with the product he/she received? It's important to keep track of what they feel about their experience with your products. After all, they are responsible for bringing in the money.

If they are not happy about the product received, you may lose their business. To ensure that your dropshipping business runs smoothly, you will have to know all the possible mistakes that could cause your business to suffer.

Dropshipping Mistakes You Should Avoid

- **Feeling Pressure Over Shipping Expenses**

Worrying too much about shipping costs will make it harder for you to run your dropshipping business. If you have to keep track of shipments from multiple sellers located in various regions, you will know that shipping prices vary in all those places.

DROPSHIPPING

That will also make it harder to set a balanced profit margin. If you are not careful here, you might end up paying more for products and shipping costs handled by your seller, leading to a low profit or even loss for you. An effective and stress-free way to deal with this issue is by keeping a flat rate for product shipping costs from all your sellers. That's how you can streamline the shipping expenses properly.

- **Relying Carelessly on Your Suppliers**

Dropshipping businesses should never be about sitting back, relaxing, and letting your vendors handle everything. Instead, it should be about knowing what, how, and when your sellers are shipping to your customers. It is also worth mentioning that vendors may run out of goods that your customers were expecting to be delivered. What are you going to do then if you just have one seller in your reach to ship the product? You will be out of resources to fulfill your customer's orders, leading to gaining a negative reputation.

You should always have a backup plan that ensures your producers never run out of products. As an insurance policy, it is better to create a contract with your sellers to ensure they understand what you expect of them. That's how you can guarantee that your business runs smoothly.

- **Believing the Business Will Provide Easy Money**

Dropshipping provides you a convenience that most eCommerce businesses might not have. But that doesn't mean you can earn easily in this business. You have to beat the competition, develop killer marketing strategies, do ample

DROPSHIPPING

research to find reliable suppliers, and develop unique planning to survive. Dropshipping requires investing time and effort. Only then will you succeed in this business.

- **Making the Ordering Process Complicated**

It will certainly be hard to keep track of orders being shipped to customers because that is usually in your seller's hands. But it's not impossible. Customers will approach your webstore only when they are guaranteed a streamlined and quick platform to place their orders. On top of that, they will want the products delivered as per the shipping date given. Your site should provide a clear shipping date estimate based on the customer's location. Additionally, make sure that you get regular updates from your suppliers regarding the orders they have shipped. Monitoring all the orders will also help you clarify any queries that your customers might have.

- **Not Enough Brand Marketing**

To ensure that customers buy from your dropshipping store and remember your products, you will want your brand to become popular among customers. Your brand name is what makes your store products visible, among other things. If your customers forget about it, you may lose potential customers.

Focus on placing your brand name in as many places as it seems to fit. Whenever orders reach customers, make sure your brand name is present on the packages and the products. Moreover, it's always a good idea to send an acknowledgment note with the product to remind your customers of your brand.

DROPSHIPPING

- **Ignoring Order Cancellations and Amendments**

Online shoppers often end up making the wrong choices with the purchase of products. As a result, you may often see a placed order is canceled or modified. You have to keep track of such activities and do the needful without wasting any time. If they have canceled an order, make sure you refund their money within the provided timeline to keep your good reputation. If they need the shipment to reach a new address, make sure you connect with the supplier to update them with the new shipping address.

Paying close attention to such activities and doing the needful can help customers rely on your webstore for their shopping. Do not feel disappointed if a customer cancels an order and buys from somewhere else. You can follow-up to apologize to them and ask for feedback. Let them know that you will improve the product's quality for future orders to ensure a satisfying experience.

- **Mishandling Lost or Damaged Goods**

If a customer has had problems with an order, he may be dissatisfied with your services. In such a situation, you want to provide an easy and quick solution for such a client instead of making it worse. To do that, you can create a handling and managing window for them to handle the issues they had with the orders. Do not just record the complaints and let them sit idle. Work on solving the issues and let your customer know that they can rely on your business once again.

- **Complications With Returned Items**

DROPSHIPPING

Customers will often return the goods and ask for refunds, if applicable. Sometimes the reasons are genuine – while at other times, it's just because they felt like returning the products. To ensure that your returns system is efficient, you and your supplier should fix a return policy that benefits you as well as your customers. If a refund is applicable, make sure it is deposited in the customer's accounts on time. Organizing such a system will make them happy and avoid any negative feedback from them.

Customer experience is important as it will decide how your business operates in the long run. Shipping, inventory management might not be your job, but you should not just ignore them completely. With proper management and planning, you can reduce such dropshipping mistakes and make your business a success.

DROPSHIPPING

CONCLUSION

By now, you will have a clear idea of what dropshipping is all about, and you can apply the various strategies to make it productive, lucrative, and worthy of a long-term investment.

Remember that it is not always possible to get profitable returns right from the start. But you can try keeping your expenditure low to balance your marketing investments. As a beginner, you will need to make things better for your clients so they can rely on your products. Impressing them will help to spread the word of your eCommerce store.

Furthermore, don't just rely on one of two strategies throughout your business cycle. You must keep experimenting with other tactics as well so that you can help your business boost its sales with increased profit margins.

Here are some tips that you can keep in mind while running your dropshipping business:

- Negotiate with your suppliers so you can have better business deals. Your aim should be to get a maximum commission margin as you grow your dropshipping business. To do that, search for manufacturers and suppliers who have great products but low sales. Such businessmen will willingly collaborate with you.

- Take out a part of your budget and invest it in your support team as well. While you might initially start the business alone, you can always make room to expand your

DROPSHIPPING

team and have them work with you. A professional team with experience may also teach you trending and effective tactics to apply to your business.

- Try to meet up with sellers who are available in your area. Being accessible to them helps you monitor your business efficiently. You can even visit them and see the quality of the products firsthand. That way, you can market the products to your potential customers with confidence.

- Remember that things will not always be great when you run a dropshipping business. Sometimes you may run out of products, and at other times, you may have a conflict with the sellers. All these problems should be dealt with without pressure by making sure they do not happen in the first place. Be alert and do not just let the business run on its own. Always be in touch with the seller to learn how they are handling the products for your customers on your behalf.

- Choose the products smartly. Do not follow the common trend as there will already be many sellers dealing with customers who need such products. If you still want to choose a category in this competitive market, you better have a decent budget to spend on the ads, webstore, and other resources you need for your business.

We hope you had a great time reading the information contained in this eBook. This book has covered all the basics that you need to know about the dropshipping business. It will be a lot to digest all the above information in one go. We suggest going through the book multiple times and referring

DROPSHIPPING

to it whenever needed in the long term. Once you apply the information, tips, and strategies in your business, you will notice how capably your webstore moves forward to generate worldwide buyers.

Made in the USA
Coppell, TX
16 September 2023

21625026R00085